The Liberal Monument

THE LIBERAL MONUMENT

URBAN DESIGN AND THE LATE MODERN PROJECT

ALEXANDER D'HOOGHE

—

PRINCETON ARCHITECTURAL PRESS, NEW YORK

in collaboration with

BERLAGE INSTITUTE, ROTTERDAM

Co-published by
—
Princeton Architectural Press
37 East 7th Street
New York, NY 10003
For a free catalog of books call
1-800-722-6657
Visit our website at www.papress.com
—
Berlage Institute
Botersloot 25
3011 HE Rotterdam
The Netherlands
www.berlage-institute.nl
—
in affiliation with
Delft University of Technology

Editor: Dan Simon
Designer: Paul Wagner
—
Special thanks to: Nettie Aljian,
Bree Anne Apperley, Sara Bader,
Nicola Bednarek, Janet Behning,
Becca Casbon, Carina Cha,
Tom Cho, Penny (Yuen Pik) Chu,
Russell Fernandez, Pete Fitzpatrick,
Jan Haux, Linda Lee, Laurie Manfra,
John Myers, Katharine Myers,
Andrew Stepanian, Jennifer Thompson,
Joseph Weston, and Deb Wood of
Princeton Architectural Press
—Kevin C. Lippert, publisher

Library of Congress
Cataloging-in-Publication Data
Hooghe, Alexander d', 1973–
The liberal monument : urban design
and the late modern project /
Alexander D'Hooghe. — 1st ed.
      p.   cm.
ISBN 978-1-56898-824-5 (alk. paper)
1. City planning—Political aspects.
2. Architecture and society—History—
20th century. I. Title. II. Title: Urban
design and the late modern project.
HT166.H662 2010
307.1'216—dc22
                            2010009122

CONTENTS

"The rule of the idea is stronger than the rule of law."
—Maxwell Fry, *The Idea and Its Realization*, 1952

THE LIBERAL MONUMENT

The city has ceased to be a figure in which the public can see
its reflection as an intact whole. The following excavates the
abandoned foundations of a project to give a form to such a public:
a template for coordinated intervention in the field of sprawl, lost
in the archives of Modernism. This book is about such a template,
called "the Group." An assembly of conflicting symbols, each a
monumental tribute to a distinct destiny, the Group offers new terms
to replace commonplaces of urban design: It is not bottom-up but
top-down, not cryptic but clear, not fabric but figure, not object but
assembled complex, not everyday but elite. The Group was first
evident in manifestoes of a "New Monumentality" (1944).[8] Today,
as in the decade preceding World War II, economic crisis spreads,
totalitarian thinking spreads, and mass regression may ensue. Read
as a symbolic form of liberalism, the Group is of shocking relevance
to our own current historical moment. Reality is grim, and we
had better act before disintegration.

　　　The project of the liberal monument proposes exactly that.
It deploys a series of civic complexes across the existing, vast
net of suburban sprawl. It makes the complexes strictly public in
nature, in opposition to the surrounding realm of private enterprise;
it constructs an aesthetic based on a tight grouping of mutually
opposing, conflicting monuments, each screaming their own desires
into the surrounding emptiness. The liberal monument would alter
the status quo of the totality of sprawl by intervening in just a
few spots. It would add a layer of choice, by introducing a system
of public architecture in a territory otherwise devoid of it.

GROUP

The formal innovation of the Liberal Monument is the Group, a template for discrete interventions, to be multiplied and distributed in the sprawl as centers of resistance against this homogenizing field, and in stark contrast to it. As such, the Group is:

1. Finite: It is a constructed monumental assemblage as opposed to a continuous, ever-growing, unconscious field of parcels and singular statements.

2. Symbolic: It asserts, through architecture, a series of ideals and visions not represented in the sprawling field.

3. Public: It is accessible to all and entices different groups. It does not have to be entirely constructed by government to achieve this.

4. Prescribed: It is itself a figure, composed of at least three elements: a platform and at least two opposing monuments in tight juxtaposition, allowing for a pedestrian experience of the group as a single space.

5. Ordering: Set in sprawl, the Group has the capacity to reorder it without destroying it. The Group is a haven. It introduces a structure into what was previously just a field.

PROTAGONISTS

Berlin, Isaiah (1909–1997), an intellectual historian and philosopher, was born in Tsarist Russia and immigrated to the UK in 1921. He taught at the University of Oxford and was the founding president of Wolfson College, Oxford. Berlin developed a political philosophy of liberalism and pluralism that traces its roots back to nineteenth-century Romanticism.

Cassirer, Ernst (1874–1945), an intellectual historian and philosopher, was born in Germany and immigrated to the United States in 1940. He taught at both Yale University and Columbia University. His magnum opus, The Philosophy of Symbolic Forms, published in German in the 1920s, is an attempt at a general theory of culture through the prism of increasing symbolic and abstract representation.

Giedion, Sigfried (1883–1968), an architectural historian, was born in Prague. He was a student of the famous Swiss art historian Heinrich Wölfflin (1864–1945) and a key figure in the Congrès International d'Architecture Moderne (CIAM) conventions from 1928 until 1953. Later he was closely associated with Walter Gropius (1883–1969). He was Lecturer in Architectural History at Harvard University from the 1930s until his death.

Kahn, Louis (1901–1974), an architect, was born in Estonia. His family emigrated to the United States in 1905. He taught architecture at MIT and at the University of Pennsylvania.

Maki, Fumihiko (b. 1928), a Pritzker Prize-winning architect, was born in Japan. He attended the Graduate School of Design at Harvard University in 1952 where he studied under Sert and Giedion. He was an assistant professor at Washington University in St. Louis from 1956 to 1961 and at the Graduate School of Design from 1962 to 1965. He returned to Japan in 1965.

Ortega y Gasset, José (1883–1955), an intellectual historian and liberal philosopher, was born in Spain. He left the country during the Spanish Civil War and went into exile in Argentina until 1945. His magnum opus, The Revolt of the Masses, was first published in 1930 in Spanish; it is a reflection on the historical development of Europe in light of its turn toward totalitarianism.

Sert, Josep Lluís (1902–1983), an architect, was born in Spain. He emigrated to the United States in 1940, where he helped publish the Athens Charter in 1942. He was chair of the 1951 CIAM conference on "The Core, about a modernist concept of urban centrality"; he also organized the first Urban Design Conference in 1956 and the first Urban Design department at the Harvard Graduate School of Design in 1959. His practice, Town Planning Associates (TPA) designed urban projects in Latin America, and buildings in Europe and North America.

URBAN DESIGN

As a meaningful practice, urban design cannot be the same as "urbanism"—a word that describes the entire sphere of practices that have produced existing urban experiences, situations, and (semi)urbanized geographic areas. Given that more than half of the world now lives in an urbanized condition, and the other half is about to join them in the next two decades, "urban" basically describes the entire universe of human existence, and "urbanism" describes that totality, as well as the project and plans that are imagined to alter or transform this status quo. "Urbanism" describes the world as it is, and also all its alternatives. Taken this way, it now means everything and its opposite. Such a word does not deserve to exist. It is wholly empty.

Urban design, then, should not compound urbanism's attempt to be everything to everyone. It needs narrow-mindedness. First, urban design describes the world not as it is, but as it should be. Reality is the field of urban studies. Aspiration is that of urban design. Second, urban design does not aim to describe that ideal scenario in its totality, but operates only on a scale which the human body and sense can experience as a whole. Beyond that scale, we find issues of landscape, territory, and planning. Third, urban design subscribes to a collectively shared physical space. It uses the scale prism to make concrete statements about the public as a whole. Beyond that are issues of architecture and interior design. An ideal, about the public as a whole, is a single spatial experience: if it sounds like a recipe for conflicts between opposing ideals, myths, and interests, that is because it is.

For that reason, urban design is always political. And since it is political, it can never obey the laws of academic well-being— which make priorities of philosophical detachment and dispassionate, value-free description. For the same reason, urban design cannot function as a professional discipline. However, by the same token, urban design is able to perform something truly amazing. Well-trimmed, freed from its obsessive desire to please everyone, it reveals itself for what it really is: a series of nonconsensual projects that translate political ideals into spatial and formal templates. In other words, urban design is the birthplace of political aesthetics. As a field, it is a collection of conflictual ideologies about the form of the collective. The Liberal Monument is but one of these ideologies, one of the first formulations of urban design as a modernist project in the mid-twentieth-century United States.

A scale comparison of Boris Iofan's Palace of the Soviets to Konstantin Thon's Cathedral of Christ the Saviour.

CENTERS OF RESISTANCE

It is necessary that the institutions of society should make provision for keeping up, in some form or other, as a corrective to partial views, and a shelter for freedom of thought and individuality of character, a perpetual and standing opposition to the will of the majority...a centre of resistance, round which all the moral and social elements which the ruling power views with disfavour may cluster themselves, and behind whose bulwarks they may find shelter from the attempts of that power to hunt them out of existence.[9]

The passage above, by the liberal political philosopher John Stuart Mill (1806–73), can be read as a call to arms for urban design to build centers of resistance against the hegemonic logics of a mass society, which continues to materialize in post–war America as sprawl. However, having witnessed the self-destruction of European mass society, the protagonists argue for a different kind of public form. This new public form is not yet in existence, it is a project. Is the project of urban design to install a liberal order on Mill's terms?

Sert, Giedion, and Kahn at first seemed to have embraced the ideal public sphere, described by seminal philosopher Immanuel Kant (1724–1804), in their frequent idealizing references to forms of ancient Greek democracy. In discussing Kant, philosopher Jürgen Habermas (b. 1929) points out that the former's ideal public sphere sees a gathering of citizens capable of engaging in calm, rational discussion toward a common purpose.[10] Because it operates in a space strictly separated from the private sphere, the public sphere is liberated to speak in a reasonable manner, whereas the private sphere (which includes religion, identity, finances, and work—all guaranteed and exercised without restraint outside of the public sphere) is understood as uncontaminated by any of these issues. Kant's bourgeois rational conversation presupposed a citizenry without financial needs but Habermas points out how the industrial

15

revolution brings new constituencies into being. These new arrivals find themselves structurally locked out of the Kantian ideal space for reason, which henceforth loses its legitimacy as a model for the public sphere. At the same time, they were suspicious of the masses' capacity to emancipate themselves and engage in "rational conversation." Europe's crisis—the barbarian regression of the 1930s—had seen matters of religion, language, nationalism, divergent belief systems, and other issues of identity, which in the Kantian *polis* were supposed to belong to the sphere of private concerns, completely inundate the public sphere. And the protagonists' project accepts this inevitable collusion by proposing to formalize the diversity of competing myths.

LIBERALISM AS FORMALISM

Against a public opinion that, as it seemed, had been perverted
from an instrument of liberation into an agent of repression,
liberalism, faithful to its own rationality, could only summon
public opinion once again. Yet what was needed now was
a restricted arrangement to secure for a public opinion finding
itself in the minority an influence against the prevailing opinions
that per se it was incapable of developing. In order to save the
principle of publicness even against the tyranny of an unenlight-
ened public opinion, it was to be augmented with elements of
representative publicness (*Öffentlichkeit*) to such an extent that
an esoteric public of representatives could emerge.[11]

Kahn is a formalist.[12] Giedion is a formalist—by virtue of his
disciplinary outlook as a former pupil of the art historian Heinrich
Wölfflin. When Sert said "We will design the container, the people
will do the rest," he was adopting a formalist stance. Is formalism
a necessary ingredient of the Liberal Monument?

A liberal philosophy of the public sphere, in and after the
arrival of mass culture, must give first priority to the principle
of representation rather than the principle of democracy. The legitimacy of the democratic state depends on the houses of parliament
forming a representation of the totality of all the individuals, commonly referred to as the public. In an ideal democracy, if that public
is stratified into different politico-cultural fields, the houses will
ideally represent this stratification accurately, thanks to the principle
of "one citizen, one vote." Notwithstanding gross simplifications
entailed by this approach, mass democracy is assumed here to
result in an accurate representation of its subjects in the parliament.
This is direct democracy, and its logic results in the legitimacy of
majority rule, or *majoritarianism*.[13]

A liberal political philosophy rejects majoritarianism. If the
results of the vote lead to a representation that certain minorities
find unsatisfactory and illegitimate, liberalism will adjust the system

so that they too find themselves represented. Examples include rules of affirmative action, strengthening the representation of women and minorities, or the historical legacy of a senate as a chamber of parliament where upper classes are represented above their numerical weight. Representation thus supersedes democracy itself as the foundational principle of a liberal concept of the public sphere. The parliament serves as a figure that crystallizes a liberal vision of the entire body of the public, and indeed of society, as a layered cake that contains different interests within itself. Alexis de Tocqueville (1805–59) observed that American democracy is a dictatorship of the middle classes:

> The very essence of democratic government consists in the absolute sovereignty of the majority; for there is nothing in democratic states that is capable of resisting it. Most of the American constitutions have sought to increase this natural strength of the majority by artificial means.[14]

On the contrary, a liberal concept of the public sphere is starkly opposed to the hegemony of one particular group, even if it constitutes a numerical majority. In the liberal figure of parliament, representation supersedes democracy. Although the liberal figure of the parliament may reduce democracy to a mere ritual, this is necessary to save the idea of democracy by protecting it against its own authoritarian impulse.

The point of this discussion is not to defend or attack liberal democracy, but merely to interpret the Group's project as a translation of a liberal conception of the public sphere into a project that, in the words of Mill, serves as a "center of resistance" against the proliferating hegemony of the middle classes. In this light, the Liberal Monument is nothing less than the symbolic form of a liberal political aesthetic. The populace is aestheticized into a grouping of icons, each representing the interest of a larger constituency. Together, these establish the contours of a public. In hindsight, we can say that the postwar urban core is a group of tightly placed yet opposing monuments; that it had become to postwar liberalism what the Soviet Palace was to Stalin, what *cardus* and *decumanus* were to the ancient Romans, and what cathedrals are to the Catholic Church. In other words, it is the symbolic form of an idealized socio-political order, captured in a formal diagram and spatialized as a microcosm of the vision for the whole.

The fundamental consistency between representation as a political concept of liberalism, and representation as an aesthetic project in the arts, is to be found in the underlying notion of formalism. Politically speaking, formalism is associated with the representation of citizens and community in institutions, while informality is associated with grassroots democracy and community life. However, the rise of the informal society in the 1960s, in opposition to society's formal structure, corresponds to a similar evolution in architectural urbanism, eloquently expressed by Bernard Rudofsky (1905–88) in Architecture Without Architects (1964).[15] Here, informality became the new dogma. Formalist architects of the 1950s—Kahn, Paul Rudolph (1918–1997), and others—were considered to be out of touch with the early 1960s reality of mass popular culture, which was associated with immediacy, informality, and a new authenticity. Yet informality also constitutes a retreat on the part of the subjects (citizens and communities), away from commitment toward a larger institutional mission to define large-scale public forms and figures. Whilst seemingly a legitimate ideological posture, the result is that such forms and figures are still being erected, albeit in a state of intellectual surrender to the negotiation between political/financial power brokers and community interests.

Formalism in the arts has historically been a movement that treats form as its own content, irrespective of the degree to which it actually represents the world of phenomena. Russian formalists of the 1920s and their early postwar American counterparts alike attempted a treatment of literature and painting as a system of forms that carry their own meaning, regardless of any interpretative apparatuses of psychology, history, or political ideology, which only yielded its derivative values but not its core structure: the form itself.[16] In philosophy, neo-Kantian formalists such as Cassirer went as far as to propose the study of scientific formulas, not as descriptions of nature, but rather as autonomous logical forms; forms whose structures are worth studying, isolated from their validation through nature.

Formalism in relation to a political philosophy of liberalism relates to the treatment of democracy as a ritual to confirm a representation that is in fact not democratic at all. Liberalism fears the tyranny of the majority, and therefore formalizes a public diversified into competing audiences. The form (or representation) of the public is independent from its actual statistical composition. This crystallization of a vast, sprawling culture into a singular precisely defined space, like the space in houses of parliament, requires the introduction of a significant formalist influence. The form of the public that is crafted here is its own content, namely liberalism itself, and democracy—the actual composition, determined by numbers (or data) of the actual totality of individuals and citizens, is a different matter.

As a result, the formalism contained in the liberal conception of the public aligns itself with the formalist device of the tight grouping of opposing monumental symbols. The latter is nothing else but the ideogram of the former. The public is constructed as a grouping of difference. Liberalism's desire to institutionalize the coexistence of incompatible entities is articulated as a political aesthetic through the device of the Group.

NOT PROGRAM BUT FLOW
BETWEEN PROGRAMS

Images reproduced courtesy Maki and Associates

The primacy of formalism corresponds to the shriveling of functionalism as a driver of urban design—a big departure within modernism
from the early years of the Athens Charter. When placed in the
context of a larger sociopolitical project, architecture and planning
have often turned to program as a prime carrier to achieve their
goals. Program refers to the set of specific functions and procedures
of private life which an architecture project establishes through its
formal layout. This can be observed in the utopian socialist settlements founded by Robert Owen (1771–1858) and Charles Fourier
(1772–1837); in the early twentieth-century idea of planning based
on functional zoning; and more recently, the Office for Metropolitan
Architecture's (OMA) definition of an architecture whose form is
driven by the layering and interlacing of different programs in the

1990s.[17] Yet, the mid-century architectural concepts that concern us here are indifferent to the content of the program. Sert's civic complex listing includes almost every imaginable program, but instead of employing the program as a social tool, he emphasized the study and manipulation of public flows. His interest was in the space *between* programs, space in which the human constituents are exposed to each other.

Maki's concepts in the early 1960s, too, focused almost exclusively on flows that relate private programs to each other. In the drawing series for Dojima (1962) in Osaka, Japan, the entire architectural agenda was boiled down to the organization of circulation in order to find a form that could structure these flows. Kahn's parking center projects for Philadelphia—he who said that "the program is nothing"—are stations that organize the transubstantiation from automobile to pedestrian.[18] The protagonists strive to stage an ideal liberal public, at a moment when traditional public spaces are evacuated and in their respective projects, the attention of urbanism shifts from program to organizational form.

In the 1950s, machineries of governance increasingly organized mass culture by means of an apparatus of organizational rules and codes, objectively confirmed in new postwar institutions such as the International Standards Organization (ISO). Architecture internalized these controls, and the increasing regimentation of functions through building/planning code, proceduralization of construction through prefabrication/economies of scale, and logistical prescription through Taylorization of interiors, left architects with fewer options to actually design.

Vanguard designers, finding themselves in a forced retreat into residual, public spaces, adopted the same organizational techniques deployed in the mainstream, but with a completely different purpose: instead of efficiency, they wanted friction; instead of smoothness, intersection. If "organization" had been the operational means of increasingly structured former private spheres through the rule of government, the protagonists' manipulation of public space uses the same language in a different sphere, for an opposite purpose: an uneasy coexistence and dysfunctional frictions, not order and efficiency.

SPRAWL

Majoritarianism (rule by the majority) is a principle that would homogenize a totality according to the views of the majority by taking the statistical middle of the curve as a universal standard. As the totality of a suburban or exurban territory where prior towns and settlements have been subjected to a systematic, singular logic of the statistical middle ground, we would argue that sprawl is a material, spatial manifestation of majoritarian rule.

THE CORE

The Core is a series of precisely circumscribed figures of publicness in the background of a (dis)urbanizing, privatized territory. It also denotes a late modernist attempt at re-inventing the historic city center as a more abstract public form, most explicitly so at the 1951 CIAM Conference with the same name. The Core project constitutes a radical departure within modernist planning, indeed, from any ambition to plan the city in its entirety. Its strategy is geared, instead, to the fragment: the civic kernel, embryo of an intense urbanity.

What began in Europe as Sert's attempt to bring moments of civilization to the regressive masses populating the European cities of the 1930s became, after traveling across the ocean to America, a project of civic moments within the expanding territory of sprawl. The realm of American private enterprise and its spatial

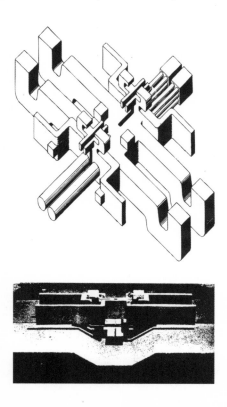

Hans Hollein, design for an interchange, 1964, as published in exhibition catalog of show at Richard Feigen Gallery, Chicago, 1969. Reprinted courtesy Atelier Hollein.

manifestation, sprawl, remained internally untouched; but an element that was missing before was introduced: limited, clearly delineated spaces of a deliberate public are to be injected at opportune places. Inside these public projects, monument groups are to articulate the forced co-existence of private interests within a single space, rather than allowing them to be merely juxtaposed and segregated by parcels, as sprawl in principle does.

Direct state control over the territorial organization—a given in most European states—is an anomaly in America, where suburbia forms a decentralized net without consciously articulated internal nodes. The Core must therefore acquire its identity as a figure against an established background, rather than be asserted as a utopian model, i.e., a wholesale oppositional alternative to the city as it is currently understood. Earlier utopian models of urbanism were perfect new societies, imbued with their own sense of order, proposed as replacements for the existing order. Compared to such models, which exist in the abstract, the figure-background aspect of the Core is a point of decisive difference. Blatantly asserting its identity in opposition to that background—which it needs as much as it needs its own content—the Core stresses its difference from existing reality by existing within it.

The Core points to the possibility of a utopian alternative to reality, but it is a symbolic tribute to utopia, rather than its enactment. The mere existence of the Core will demonstrate the possibility of an alternative order. Insofar as each instance of the Core is a symbolic microcity—a small-scale model of what a liberal society might look like—its architecture contains a broader imagination of a different societal geography. The Core is essentially a constructivist project, not in a stylistic sense, but in its fundamental aspiration to heroically construct—against the forces of nature, history, and economy—a definition of civilization: against nature, the decision to build an artificial, protected empty space; against history, the decision that a city center needs no century-long accumulation of identity, but rather can be produced by sheer force of will; and against economy and capital, the decision to invest in a statement about the collective.

SERT'S CORE

CIAM 8

In a 1953 speech, Sert observed the weakness of the architectural object, which has been disarmed by the overwhelming scale of what surrounds it: infrastructures, networks, and mass productions.[19] The city had bypassed the architectural object. To succeed in the heroic re-conquest of semi-urbanized territories of sprawl, a more powerful device will be necessary. The civic complex, or Core, is his proposal. The Core is larger than a building, but the difference is not just a question of size. A proper Core must consist of various objects and define the space between them. It will entail the creation of a pedestrian environment, united by a systematic spectacle of abstract art, and by a greater density than the surrounding automobile-driven suburb.

Sert's Core is to be made up of formations that are abstract, and therefore semiotically inexhaustible and open to multiple interpretations. As a constitutive fragment to the city at large, proposed as an alternative to planning a city in its totality, the Core is a significant departure from the functional city paradigm associated with the Athens Charter.

Early Enlightenment thought equates nature with enlightenment, and the influence of nature on man with a turn toward a more free and egalitarian society. For Thomas Jefferson (1743–1826), and later for the American architect Frank Lloyd Wright (1867–1959), evil was in the city, which eradicated humanism. Sert and

Image logo of the proceedings of the 1951 CIAM (Conference on the heart of the city).

José Ortega y Gasset (1883–1955) reached an opposite conclusion, equating civility with urbanity: The intelligence of man is based on his separation, or walling-off of himself, from nature. From Sert's point of view, the sprawling of America, due to a popular underwriting of the Jeffersonian bucolic vision, threatened a degeneration into barbarism. Accordingly, the Core, as the introduction of large-scale dense development, is an effort to bring civility to the sprawling city. To this end, Sert's project bridges different scales, from planningto architecture, finally arriving at an intermediate scale of operation: that of the Core. In his case, this is a single main core with smaller subsidiaries. This renewed celebration of metropolitan urbanity will instill the values of a liberal idea of publicness in the citizens. This celebration and its intention will acquire form through the grouping of sculptural forms in such a way as to establish a formal spatial principle of public space as interstitial, as existing in the cracks of established networks, social formations, and institutions. The idea of the Core—the notion of the intermediate scale and interstitial space—would survive to become one of the most common descriptions for the field of urban design.

ON THE LARGE CIVIC COMPLEX

Sert:
One of the greatest challenges for architects is the
carrying out of large civic complexes: the integration
of city-planning, architecture, and landscape architecture; the building of a complete environment. This is
a vast and ambitious task. We should be aware of that
fact and of all barriers and limitations that lie in
between...contemporary architecture as a style is still
in its beginnings; the search for a more complete architectural vocabulary, a more satisfactory expression,
should continue....Architects should decide, together
with city planners, to invade the no-man's land of civic
design....I call this field a no-man's land because
contemporary architecture and planning have not developed in it and it offers no really full size example of a
complete civic complex that can give us a picture of an
entire civic environment, where architecture is at its
best in true relation to open areas and traffic networks
can be shown as an example of what the city centers of our
time can be. Up to now, contemporary architecture has
produced at its best a few scattered good examples of
isolated buildings. But much of the more recent work...
will be absorbed by an overpowering, hostile environment:
the chaotic streets, the creeping blight, and the slums
of our cities. This culture of ours is a culture of
cities, a civic culture...where the landscape is really
a man-made landscape...it is where city planning and
architecture are at their best. No isolated building can
compete with them.[20]

Ortega y Gasset:
For in truth the most accurate definition of the urbs
(city) and the polis (citizenship) is very like the comic
definition of a cannon. You take a hole, wrap some steel
wire tightly round it, and that's your cannon. So, the

urbs and polis start by being an empty space, the forum, the agora, and all the rest are just a means of fixing that empty space, of limiting its outlines. The polis is not primarily a collection of habitable dwellings, but a meeting place for citizens, a space set apart for public functions. The city is not built, as is the cottage or the domus (house), to shelter from the weather and to propagate the species—these are personal, family concerns—but in order to discuss public affairs. Observe that this signifies nothing less than the invention of a new kind of space, much more new than the space of Einstein. Till then only one space existed, that of the open country, with all the consequences that this involves for the existence of man. The man of the fields is still a sort of vegetable. . . . How is this possible? How can man withdraw himself from the fields? Where will he go, since the earth is one huge, unbounded field? Quite simply, he will mark off a portion of this field by means of walls, which set up an enclosed finite space over amorphous, limitless space. Here you have the public square. It is not, like the house, an 'interior' shut in from above, as are the caves which exist in the fields, it is purely and simply the *negation of the fields*. The square, thanks to the walls which enclose it, is a portion of the countryside which turns its back on the rest, eliminates the rest, and sets up in opposition with it. This lesser rebellious field, which secedes from the limitless one, and keeps to itself, is a space sui generis, of the most novel kind, in which man frees himself from the community of the plant and the animal, leaves them outside, and creates an enclosure apart which is purely human, a civil space.[21]

POLYNUCLEARITY

The cure for our widespread, amorphous modern cities is more readily achieved by the creation of new cores—new concentrations of activity—that express the special values of each scale or grouping, than by endeavoring to slice the whole area into village neighborhoods: by a visual emphasis upon centers of integration rather than upon bands of separation.[22]

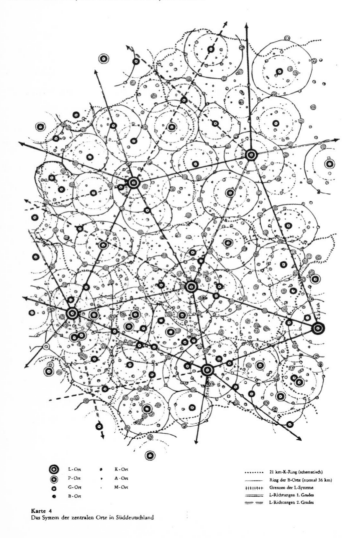

⊚ L-Ort	• K-Ort	········	21 km-K-Ring (schematisch)
⊚ P-Ort	⁜ A-Ort	———	Ring der B-Orte (normal 36 km)
⊙ G-Ort	· M-Ort	┼┼┼┼┼┼	Grenzen der L-Systeme
• B-Ort		══════	L-Richtungen 1. Grades
		═ ═ ═	L-Richtungen 2. Grades

Karte 4
Das System der zentralen Orte in Süddeutschland

British planner Jacqueline Tyrwhitt (1905–83) was a con-
temproary of Sert and Giedion, teaching and organizing at Harvard
in the same period. She argued that the city-suburb system should
become polynuclear. During the Core conference, she argued
against a classification of cores on the basis of scale (small cores
for the neighborhood, one big core for the city at large), instead
favoring a constellation of cores to operate on the level of the entire
city, each with a different programmatic identity: public administration, entertainment-oriented, business-oriented, etc. In this way,
she moved beyond Sert, who was never capable of transcending
his own superficial reading of the single-core historic city—an idée
fixe destroyed later by planning theorists like Hans Blumenfeld
(1892–1988), who showed that older historic cities such as London
had a polynuclear structure.[23] Tyrwhitt sketches a constellation of
cores, a net cast over the sprawling region, implying new nuclei
where there was previously only sprawling formlessness. Instead of
re-urbanization, she concentrated moments of metropolitanism in
a net of dispersed nuclei. Tyrwhitt's turnabout constitutes a fundamental reformatting of the Core on the basis of an acceptance of the
suburban condition rather than its denial. She describes a constellation of architectural interventions meant as cores for the suburbs.
The consequence is that the historic city center can simply become
one core among many, in a dynamically, ever-further expanding
system of gravity points in suburban sprawl. From that perspective, the reductionist identification of the Core with the wave of the
urban renewal that has harshly transformed America's historic city
centers—a prevalent interpretation today—is factually incorrect.

Tyrwhitt was a student of the Scottish urbanist Patrick Geddes
(1854–1932), whose Garden City diagrams articulated an exodus
from the city into the territories of nature, dotted with occasional
villages.[24] However, the reality on the ground throughout the 1950s
was that the exodus from the city did not result in villages but
rather in quasi-continuous territories of sprawl. Tyrwhitt accepted
this condition as it was, but re-projected the diagram over it. Hers
are not villages amidst nature but high-density urban civic complexes amidst a sprawl carpet. Not community but urbanity, not
amidst nature but amidst second nature, her proposal inverts the

fundamental premise of both the anti-urban Garden City and the pro-urban drive of Sert.

Tyrwhitt realized that the Core project might not require a centralized hierarchical planning system. As a student at the University of Berlin–Charlottenburg in 1936–7, she was exposed to the German geographer Walter Christaller's (1893–1969) "central place" theory.[25] Christaller had postulated in 1933 that protocapitalism had an inherent tendency to polycentric organization, as could be seen in the distances between cities, towns, and hamlets over a wide territory in southern Germany. By 1941, the German economist August Lösch (1906–45) would extend Christaller's ideas to assert that a polycentric logic also structures the development pattern within metropolitan areas.[26] This theory provided the contours for Tyrwhitt's own proposal, but while the Christaller-Lösch theorem was fundamentally descriptive, in Tyrwhitt's hands it became a project for the transformation of the suburbs.[27]

ORGANIZING DISTANCES

In 1999, the problem of sprawl, or the peripheries, was placed front and center in a theme issue of *Urbanismo Revista* edited by the Spanish architect Manuel de Sola-Morales (b. 1939), himself a student of Sert and Giedion. This marked the beginning of two decades of Western European self-discovery of its increasingly suburban, sprawling development patterns.[28] The critical difference between this and the dozens of other publications about European sprawl—many of them impressionistic journeys that end up justifying the status quo of sprawl—is that Sola-Morales made the search for a new logic of interventions his central aim. Reflecting its activist nature, the issue was called, "Periphery as a Project." Sola-Morales claimed that the spatial principle of sprawl was that of organizing distances. If the historic European city became legible, it was because of continuities that were established by sheer building mass. This was why, for Sola-Morales, the longitudinal section was the prime medium for the study of intervention in this apparatus. In sprawl, this principle is reversed. The open areas between developments establish the visibility of each development, define what is object and what is not, and give renewed force to the markers of settlement by placing them on the background of a fundamentally white empty canvas.

Jan van Eyck, The Adoration of Mystic Lamb, 1432, taken from the Ghent Altarpiece, Ghent, the Netherlands

Sola-Morales's net of distances refers to the physical geography of late-medieval Europe. In northern France and Flanders, for example, flatlands were punctuated by a series of Gothic church towers that dwarfed the remainder of each town and allowed it to blend into the land from a distance. These towers recur in a triangular pattern, and the distances of eight to ten miles (twelve to fifteen kilometers) between towns corresponds to the time it took to walk from one market to the next and back within a single day.

Sola-Morales's discussion appealed for a model of intervention that would resurrect what he called a "Gothic model of space," a framework for testing proposals that would favor clusters of buildings, however insecure and open. These would be urban groupings of diverse forms, with enough formal personality to carry symbolic value and ordering potential, even in isolation. They would enable the observer to understand the territory as a landscape form that is subject to very strict ecological and environmental demands. More specifically, this model of settlement would support appreciation of the void and the interstitial lands as positive material. Sola-Morales continues:

> Maybe we are today returning to a "gothic" model of space.
> It is the loss of classical (Roman) regularity in urbanism which
> wishes to be modern and still needs regularities (of scale,
> volume, material, and use). A non-regularity however, governed
> from within itself by the law of the mutual distances as its main
> regulator, rather than thought through from above or from
> outside. The urbanism of the periphery may involve a sequence
> of groupings built by induction and by dialogue: in this field
> deduction is always thwarted.[29]

The reader will be struck by the dramatic similarity in the language of Sola-Morales's description of the project for the peripheries, and the language of Sert and other protagonists for the Core. Both talk about groupings, assemblages of symbolic forms, and the distances between which establish a constellation. Strikingly, we have come full circle. Sola-Morales is critical of Sert and Giedion, whom he finds theological and dogmatic, and seeks a contextual intelligence as an alternative.[30] But when it comes to addressing sprawl, Sola-Morales intuitively returned to template-based thinking and embraced some principles of the Sertian Core.

A FORMAL TEMPLATE FOR THE CORE

The Group is a gathering of independent, sculptural, monumental forms of architecture, landscape, and infrastructure: buildings, open spaces, and artworks, placed in proximity to one another to create intimate interstitial spaces. The scale of the Group never exceeds that of a pedestrian's walking radius, within which it generates a sense of centrality. Within the Group, the exact center is in the vicinity but always fleeting, always where one is not. Perception of the Group oscillates between a grasp of the whole and a recognition of its radically different individual elements. There is no synthesis; each form remains visible independently. Sert's group (1951), Giedion's group design (1957), and Maki's group form (1961) plus the unnamed pattern that emerged in Kahn's urban design in Philadelphia, provide examples through which a formal template for the Core can be understood.

EMPTY SPACE

Giedion presented the Swiss-French architect Le Corbusier's (1887–1965) project (1945) for Saint-Dié, France as the first manifestation of group design on an urban scale. Separated from the rest of the city, the new core for an old town sits on a vast platform, hosting an arrangement of monumental fragments. A clue to the origins of such a proposition—so different from Le Corbusier's previous urban plans, Plan Obus (1932–1942) and Ville Radieuse (1935)— is found in his entry for the first Soviet Palace competition in 1931. In that project, Le Corbusier arrived at an assembly of diverse forms by allocating different required functions into discrete forms.

The Soviet Palace competition brief called for monumental architecture. Not only does it divide up the palace program into four distinct segments, it also provided for the accommodation of large processions that would march through the palace. Le Corbusier's studies show a variety of assemblages of the same forms, with each component of the grouping serving as the functional embodiment of its program. In the final project, two major halls, spaced far apart, were connected by a long skywalk to which several minor programs were attached. Thus, he arrived at his conclusion by following a functional logic. In his proposal, the functional demand for large-scale parades through the project defies conventional urban dimensions and introduces, instead, a gigantic open space in the middle. This open space serves to destroy the probable hegemony of the biggest program chunk: the Soviet meeting hall. The parade path was not an axis but an open field. It was to become the platform. In effect, Le Corbusier used the demand for parades to destroy the Stalinist desire for an architectural megalith, using the open space to install a plurality of forms.

The palace elements are pulled even farther apart in the project for Saint-Dié, France (1945). The fragments of a composed Soviet palace are now scattered over a horizontal public platform, separated from each other by vast open space. Only in later iterations will the fragments get closer to each other.

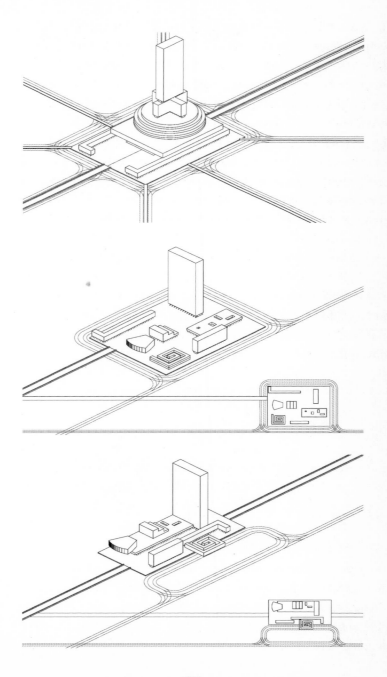

PLATFORM

The platform is a bounded, enclosed, and empty space populated by monumental symbols. In the aforementioned early versions, platforms are vast and the open spaces enormous. Mass parades are fundamentally a problem of dimensions: they require open spaces, and during off-time—that is, most of the time—they are hardscape deserts whose scale relates to the sublime and the abstract, not the conventions of the urban and the civic. A tension structures the urban design work: on one hand, the bounded platform as primal figure; on the other hand, a grouping of monuments dense enough to host a pleasant public flow of people, yet open enough not to destroy the sublime power of emptiness.

The most evident resolution of this scale problem might seem to be to further densify by increasing the number of monuments on the platform, or reducing the platform size. For example, Sert's project for Boston University (1959) increased the number of monuments on the platform. We still find the different abstract symbols of Saint-Dié: tower, slab, low building, and trapezium-shaped shell with auditorium.

Sert's Boston University campus, along the Charles River

However, the elements have approached each other, and the platform has shrunk. As a result, the big open spaces narrowed into passages, plazas, and courtyards. The ground-floor skin is often of glass, exposing elevator shafts, stairwells, and sanitary equipment. As a result, outdoors and indoors appear almost as one, reintroducing the concept of the platform after all. A few of the open spaces still frame views of the surrounding city.

Le Corbusier's 1949 proposal for the United Nations Headquarters in New York completely collapses the open space into mere expansion joints between various parts of one megabuilding. The forms touch, interpenetrate, and collide with one another. The grouping becomes, once again, a single building with several constituent forms. An institution of internationalism (like the Soviet Palace), the UN Headquarters aspired to overcome historical differences in a contemporary synthesis, and added a new chapter to the evolution of the Core: the shattered pieces have been regrouped and effectively glued back together.

In the Cidade Dos Motores, Brazil (1944) by Sert and Paul Lester Wiener (1895–1967), the platform becomes an enormous rectangular roof, punctuated by courtyards and crossed by public paths, that covers a maze of civic and entertainment programs. The roof structure provides cover from the sun and incorporates a series of dispersed elements below, a flexible accumulation of expressive forms and programs. Thus, the platform is turned upside down and becomes the roof of an enormous shed building. The zenith of civic building culture is suddenly a big box, and the monuments have become semi-interior elements. Sert did not pursue this interpretation any further.

SHATTERING AND REGROUPING

Picture of Giacometti's Projet Pour Une Place (1930–31, destroyed), as published in Giedion's Architecture and the Phenomena of Transition.

By analogy to surrealist sculpture, the prefiguration of the public, established through the interaction and space between the monuments of the group, requires the creative, semantic labor of an observer. Giedion introduced "Group Design," the last chapter of the third volume of Architecture and the Phenomena of Transition, with a photograph of Alberto Giacometti's Projet Pour Une Place (1930–31). The sculpture features a platform with four oddly curved objects standing upright, complemented by two distortions of the platform itself, similar in dimension to the four objects. Lacking a rigid geometrical order, the configuration of the six forms appears unstable and seemingly random. It is an assemblage of figures, each distinct yet each holding the others in balance. Giacometti produced this piece during his exploration of the surrealist technique of assemblage.

 Surrealist practices embraced assemblage as an alternative to conventional narrative structure. Whereas narrative is syntactical, relating the different elements into a continuity that supersedes its constituent elements, establishing a new semantic whole, the assemblage is a paratactic composition—a simple juxtaposition of elements without explicit reference to sequence, hierarchy, or other kinds of relation called up by proximity.[31] The paratactic organization implies a third term between any two juxtaposed elements—a term which, while not articulated by the artist, is filled in and called up by the observer.[32] In the observing mind, an interstitial space is defined. Though not explicitly postulated, the form of such a space emerges anew, nevertheless. Each time the observer witnesses the assemblage, he revisits an inexhaustible fund of interpretations. This in-between space is the purpose of the assemblage.

Surrealist sculpture began to appear only after Sigmund Freud (1856–1939) pioneered psychoanalysis in the early twentieth century. The medium borrowed from Freud's division of the psyche, demonstrating an acceptance of the structural incompatibility between different parts of the self—id, ego, superego. Accordingly, just as the artist's ego can abandon its attempts at synthesis, so can urbanism abandon its aspiration to a collective form, and pay tribute instead to the contradicting desires and wills between which a space of friction is established. In the Group, exposure of inconsistencies—presented as negative in surrealism—is reformulated as positive. Assembly replaces assemblage, and unification is replaced by a tribute to the vitality of negotiated conflict.

The prefiguration of the public pursued in the Core is born from the creative, semantic labor of the observer, who defines interstitial space that has not explicitly postulated its own form. This form emerges anew every time the observer witnesses the assemblage, opening an inexhaustible source of interpretations. The art historian Rosalind Krauss (b. 1941) discussed such a concept of "spacing" in her analysis of surrealist photomontage:

> Spacing destroys simultaneous presence: for it shows things sequentially, either one after another or external to one another—occupying separate cells. It is spacing that makes it clear—as it was to Heartfield, Tretyakov, Brecht, Aragon—that we are not looking at reality, but at the world infested by interpretation or signification, which is to say, reality distended by the gaps or blanks which are the formal preconditions of the sign.[33]

The modernity of the experience is no longer within the object, which can be a fossil or a historical artifact, but in the spacing that

takes it out of its conventional (or vernacular) context, and necessi-
tates a moment of interpretation on behalf of the observer. Spacing
makes the observer aware of having entered the realm of representation. Krauss's spacing gives to public space its concept. It reminds
us that the postwar return to formal urbanism in the United States
happens on terms that are radically different from the last such
iteration. Under the leadership of architects such as Daniel Burnham
(1846–1912) in Chicago, the "City Beautiful" movement aimed
to introduce formalist urbanism as Neoclassicist urbanism on an
American scale, with grand centralizing axes, symmetries, and other
classicist geometries. This large-scale Neoclassicism displayed dis-
turbing similarities to that of Europe's prewar totalitarian regimes.

Two projects for a palace, both proposed in 1934, elucidate
how the return to formalism in planning coincided with a complete
reversal of its devices. In Giacometti's sculpture Palace at 4 A.M.,
a number of sculptural forms appear in incoherent combination, not
juxtaposed on a platform but hung at different heights, resembling
a dented birdcage. This shattering and regrouping of the elements
of the classical composition, a hitherto monolithic structure,
may be read as a powerful counter-argument to a hegemonic unitary
megaobject in architecture. Contrasted with Boris Iofan's Soviet
Palace design (see The Conversation), in which ideas of classical balance and compositional wholeness are joined in an attempt
to synthesize diversity in the face of modern rupture, Giacometti's

42

sculpture constitutes a formal opposite that can be construed as a symbol of an ideological opposite. Giacometti's sculpture, and its title, allegorically suggest that a ruler who dominates and unifies everything under his command will be haunted at night by disunity and fragmentation, as the ghosts of his nightmares come to confirm all the contradictions that persist beneath the surface.

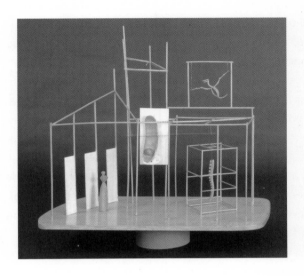

MAKI'S "MASTER FORM"

Unlike our other protagonists, Maki was not after a static composition but a flexible order that accommodates change. The master form, Maki suggested, is merely the contour of an overall form—not an actual object, but its shimmering suggestion, presented through a series of fragments. Outlining a repertoire to achieve master form, Maki proposed to arrange a series of independent elements into an open framework. Change is not a matter of naive aestheticization, but rather of the integration of modern logics of urban development. There is no need for a tabula rasa. By virtue of the repetition and variation inherent in master form, the architectural object is just one of many elements, including platforms, infrastructure, entrance systems, and topographies. This repertoire can easily be deployed onto a piece of already-occupied territory. The elements of master form do not presuppose a greenfield tabula rasa; rather, they are conceived to intervene in a half-urbanized continuum.

Maki was the first late-Modernist architect to come to terms with urban design's inevitable accommodation of reality as it exists, not only outside the perimeter of intervention, but precisely within its own template. He stressed the relevance of his formal language for society as a whole. The master form must be an objective symbol of society's underlying ideals, an embodiment of the collective content of a society. He wrote, "As soon as a form is invented, it becomes the property of society. One might almost say that it was the property of society before its discovery. A design, on the other hand, belongs to the designer."[34] Master form is a tool to supersede a designer's subjective drive and autobiographical predispositions, to arrive at a higher, more objective level of representation of the collective.

MAKI'S MASTER FORM

Maki's principles of form operationalize architect
Kevin Lynch's (1918–1984) five principles of legibility
of the city. While Maki did not refer to Lynch explicitly, his categories of collective form bear an uncanny
resemblance to the five categories of abstract cognition
described in <u>The Image of the City</u> (1961), Lynch's
investigation into the role of cognitive structures
in the process of understanding the city. Lynch concluded
that the mind attempts to understand urban experience
by creating mental maps that rely on five preeminent
categories: the landmark, the path, the district, the
node, and the edge. Maki combined his categories of
perception into a theory of operation. Like Lynch, Maki
eschewed a top-down planview of the city in favor of an
experience-oriented perspective from within.

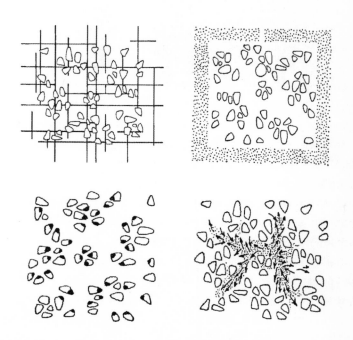

MOVING BEYOND THE TOTALIZING AMBITIONS OF URBAN PLANNING DESIGN

In the course of explaining master form, Maki cites the idea of open aesthetics, which he drew from mid-century British architect John Voelcker (1927–1972): "In open aesthetics, form is a master key, not of any aesthetical significance in itself, though capable of reciprocating the constant change of life...open aesthetics is the living extension of functionalism."

Images on this and next page, reproduced courtesy Maki and Associates

To a present-day reader, Voelcker's idea recalls the Italian writer Umberto Eco's (b. 1932) concept of the open work. Eco's book Open Work (1962) elaborates an aesthetic theory of Modernism in literature applicable to group form. Modernist abstraction, searching for a new richness of experience within a medium, demands an act of interpretation by the beholder. Eco posited that inexhaustibility of interpretation is the fundamental constitution of the open aesthetic in Modernism. The open work does not impose itself on the public, but, to the contrary, is constructed by it through a series of differing interpretations, of indefinite duration.

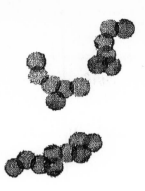

Maki may have intuitively stumbled upon a fundamental problem of urban design in a liberal democracy. A work of art is a totality, using a necessary set of codes to capture the world; but when art is urbanism, the totality of the artwork can easily come to signify the totalizing ambition of a ruler. Unlike art, urban design is burdened by complicity with politics. Maki resolved this problem by assembling a plurality of absolute statements into a group. By its association with others, each is denied its predisposition to signify a singular regime—aesthetic *or* political. The need for an overall formal proposition is as important as ever, but the urban designer must stop short of providing a literal one. As a contour, a template, the master form achieves a level of abstraction that cannot be achieved within the concrete field of architecture, but can only emerge in the interplay of forms. This technique allows a prefiguration of the collective, of the public. The utopian promise remains vital, not consumed or exhausted.

UMBERTO ECO'S <u>OPEN WORK</u>

A narrative structure must remain below all the interpretations it may elicit, but he [Alain Robbe-Grillet (1922–2008)] is wrong in thinking that it can entirely avoid them because it is extraneous to them. It can't be extraneous to them, since it is a sort of propositional function, which can stand for a series of situations that are already familiar to us. Narrative structures have become fields of possibilities precisely because, when we enter a contradictory situation in order to understand it, the tendencies of such a situation can no longer assume a unilinear development that can be determined a priori. Rather, all of them appear to us as equally possible, some in a positive fashion and some in a negative, some as a way out of the situation and others as a form of alienation to the crisis itself.[35]

THE "NOT YET" FORM

The labor of Sert, Giedion, and Maki toward the definition of a group form template remains incomplete. However, it can be said that by layering their various interpretations, both in writing and in drawings, one finds outlines for an aesthetic theory of urban design. The group form is a third realm between the fabric of the city and the monument. As an assemblage of objects on a platform, it is a symbolic gathering, an embrace, a conversation between fragments.

Group form is a dismissal of the architectural megaobject, the desperate, heroic attempt to synthesize massive amounts of program into a single gesture of the architectural object: Iofan's Soviet Palace, post–World War II megastructure dreams, etc. The Group dismisses the notion of the fabric—the formal expression of an organically growing and incrementally ordered community—in which the aspirations of individual and community are in harmony. But its own assertion remains hopeful: Its intention is to formalize the liberal vision of the public sphere by reconfiguring the public into a plurality of constituencies. It thereby installs, within its form, an intention for pluralism.

The grouping is not smooth, on the contrary, it is built of internal oppositions and does not culminate in a formal synthesis. Just as a word in a language acquires its meaning through its difference from other words, so in the Group the formal content of each constituent form is visible only through its difference from others. The assembly affords the representation of irresolvable difference. In the suburban context, such a grouping of incompatible terms has to be artificially created. Accordingly, the monuments of the Group set up no centralized view corridor, but rather intersecting sight lines to each other and to the territory beyond themselves. The center of the Group is fleeting: always near you, yet always where you are not.

Maki's "Not Yet"—so-called by British architect and writer Kenneth Frampton at Maki's Pritzker Prize ceremony in

1993—corresponds to the prefiguration of the public that was the
initial agenda of the Core.[36] A gathering of symbols and gestures
that establish a dialogue in the space between them, the master
form's elements never merge to become either a fabric or a single
object. The contours of Maki's unachieved collective object can be
imagined by extrapolating the role of the various constituents of
the Group. But the totality and synthesis of the group form is never
explicitly postulated, and so the group form does not symbolize
the foreclosure of a more integrated public. Group form denies the
public its unification, yet holds out a promise for the possibility of
just that: a prefiguration, through the contours of a master form,
whose concrete realization remains behind the horizon. Therefore,
the group is a "Not Yet" form. It invokes Ernst Bloch's (1885–1977)
"Not Yet" (the sort of promised-yet-deferred utopia, referenced
by Frampton) as well as the precepts of gestalt theory (sidebar),
both circulated for the first time in the 1950s.

GESTALT THEORY

Formal synthesis, or the merger of constituent elements
into an overall composition, has been studied in the
psychology of perception, especially in gestalt theory.
Gestalt theory occupies itself with identifying the a
priori rules that allow us to discern, in what enters
the retina as a chaotic field of stimuli, order and
overall form. Research has been conducted by presenting
subjects with random fields of dots, in which they were
consequently asked to discover a form. Gestalt theorists
claim that the subject merely constructs forms out
of these dots based on innate perceptional rules. The
influence of gestalt theory on the protagonists may be
seen in Maki's work on linkage. The essential feature
here is Maki's conception of collective form as an
incomplete figure. His project used gestalt categories
to merely suggest (but not state explicitly) an emerging
master form. He refused to deploy these categories for

50

the benefit of the whole if it caused detriment
to the individual parts. Consequently, he never made
the overall form unequivocally clear. It still has
to be constructed by the observer.

LIBERALISM

You cannot be both a liberal and a democrat, you cannot be a liberal and a despot, and you certainly cannot be a relativist. A liberal outlook assumes that each group believes absolutely in its own ideals, yet accepts that other groups do the same, leading to societal survival through a series of truces. The word "liberal," in the American context, now negatively connotes pro-big-government, anti-traditional values, and relativism. This is extremely strange given that the American founding fathers, the ultimate traditionalists, embraced several fundamental tenets of a liberal political philosophy. In Europe, "liberal" has come to be associated with "neoliberal," implying the hegemony of free markets, or in other words the belief that markets know best, being guided indirectly by an invisible hand constituted by the collective decision-making of their participants. Both meanings are slippery and, frankly, when placed in the line of the historical development of the political philosophy of liberalism, inadequate. De Tocqueville argued for liberalism as a consequence of Enlightenment thinking; political philosopher Isaiah Berlin described liberalism through the opposite perspective, Romanticism. Both views share a desire to at once-erect centers of power and simultaneously fragment them into a plurality of incompatible viewpoints. Furthermore, liberalism aspires to institutionalize these incompatible terms or, in architectural terms, to formalize them. In other words, liberalism erects institutional power only in order to fragment it immediately.

We can summarily describe liberalism by opposing it with totalitarianism (the all-embracing state). More poignantly, it also radically differs from a common interpretation of democracy called majoritarianism. Majoritarianism is an interpretation of democracy inscribed into most democratic constitutions of Western countries. It defines democratic legitimacy as political government supported by half of the votes—plus one. A genuinely liberal outlook must describe such a view as the tyranny of the majority. To save us from the dictates of a statistical summary ruling the state (in architecture, the most commonly acceptable taste), liberalism in urban design points to the installation of centers of resistance to draw power away from the hegemony of the majority, to install a plurality of power centers instead, to guarantee the representation of minorities, be they oppressed classes or "elites."

A ROMANTIC CONCEPTION OF THE PUBLIC

Berlin devoted his life to studying a counter-Enlightenment movement which, he argued, rose out of German Romanticism in the late
eighteenth century as a response to the oppressive, universalizing
rationality of the Enlightenment. It gave birth, ultimately, to a liberal
political philosophy. Contrary to many postwar German philosophers such as Habermas, Berlin saw Romanticism not as the cause
of Europe's regression, but rather as its possible redemption.[37]
Most importantly, however, he asserted that the Romantic will and
the myths it erects are not only absolutely foundational to one's
existence, they are also numerous, often mutually exclusive, and
perennially incompatible. He shattered Kant's public sphere of calm,
rational discussion for good.

Berlin rejected any idea of a public unified through reason,
instead preferring an uneasy, perpetually renegotiated coexistence
of constituencies, which could not be unified without resulting in a
totalitarianism that would eradicate the basic values of humanism.
For Berlin, then, the project of Romanticism also required, from
each belief system's point of view, a will to awareness and understanding of other points of view. Each entity broadcasts its own
truth; the figure of the public consists of the simultaneity of different,
contradicting entities, each screaming into emptiness, yet for their
very survival are forced into constant negotiation. Such a vision
uncannily resembles the project of a constellation of civic complexes
or centers of resistance, each public and thus accessible in its own
right, proclaiming a different ideal. From each complex, you have
purview on adjacent ones; at each complex, you stage the public in a
different form. The profoundness of Berlin's intellectual revolution,
from an urban-design perspective, lay in the fact that a neutral public
space disappears. Sert, Giedion, and Kahn developed their work in
the postwar climate of opinions in which Berlin—along with Karl
Popper (1902–1994), Ortega y Gasset, and Marxist philosophers

like Theodor Adorno (1903–1969) and Max Horkheimer (1895–1973)—set out to investigate the extent to which the evil that totalitarian Europe (the Nazis, Fascists, and Soviets) wrought had been called up by the project of Western philosophy itself.

The protagonists are also familiar with Cassirer, whose work on symbolic form and myth was influential throughout the 1950s. Cassirer's The Myth of the State (posthumously published in 1946) was prescient of Berlin's political philosophy as published from 1958 onwards.[38] Rather than blaming Romanticism itself, Cassirer and Berlin blamed the notion of the state as its own independent apparatus, with a power that was autonomous from the society it establishes. This idea was first established by Niccolò Machiavelli (1469–1527), but powerfully reasserted in the German political philosopher G. W. F. Hegel's (1770–1831) doctrine of the state, which in turn profoundly influenced the thought of Modern luminary Karl Marx.

The autonomous state institutionalizes the rational conversation of the Enlightenment public into a technocratic apparatus that can exist independent of the private interests of various groups. However, a crisis in the private sphere can easily destroy the legitimacy of such a state. At such a moment, Cassirer asserted, a Romantic conception of identity will be politicized on the level of the state, giving rise to modern fascism. Myth, which he defines as "the collective desire personified into certain objects," is now consciously personified into the state, and from there its mythical identity is disseminated amongst its subjects and legitimizes its own continued possession of power.[39] Furthermore, myth has the quality of dissolving all boundaries and presenting the world as an essential organic unity. Consequently, the autonomous state becomes a totalitarian state, the separation between a private and a public sphere disappears. Everything is inundated with myth.

Cassirer's analysis was not alone in adopting this position. In "Philosophy and Government Repression" and "The Greatest Danger: The State," Berlin and (respectively) Ortega y Gasset not only destroyed the unified public but also its institutional corollary, the autonomous state.[40] These liberal philosophers constructed the public as a constellation of constituencies, forcing a staged negotiation of conflicting ideals, thus reestablishing the separation between private and public spheres.

By analogy, the project of liberalism in the spirit of Mill, Berlin, and Ortega y Gasset entails the crafting of centers of resistance, each of which proclaims a different ideal. The space in between is then charged with a negotiation between these statements. The protagonists abandon any ambition to plan the totality of the city, thus invading the private sphere by the public authority (all recommended in the Athens Charter) in favor of a series of strategic interventions that left most private land untouched, and focusing the efforts of the welfare state onto a few strategic spots where they accommodate and stimulate a sense of publicness as a staging area for the battle between competing visions. And how else should we understand Sert's project for metropolitan urbanity? The common argument emerging, while not explicitly stated, is that one has to work through a series of incompatible myths to get out on the other side into a more radically rational conception of the public. Ultimately, the liberal ideal replaces the master plan (for a rational order) with a series of public projects on a background of private hegemony. From this follows a redefined need for formalism.

ROMANTIC PLURALISM

Berlin often invoked the "uneasy coexistence of incompatible terms," a concept critical to his political philosophy of liberalism. It is aptly applied to the formalist architectural concept of group form. Berlin's pluralism is derived from two axioms: communities strive toward overarching synthesis through the production of mythologies that reinforce their desires and utopias; but any overarching synthesis equals tyranny. An ethical dilemma results: pluralism is Berlin's proposed way out. Berlin discarded all attempts to achieve utopianism, replacing them with a concept of empathy. Given that there are many ideals, often incompatible to each other, humanism is reduced to the building of truces, achieved by an emphatic understanding of opposite viewpoints, without ever leading to a change in position. To understand Berlin's conception of pluralism, it is important to realize that he placed it squarely in the lineage of the Romantics such as the pioneer of *Sturm und Drang*, Johann G. Herder (1744–1803), Wolfgang Goethe (1749–1832), and Johann G. Fichte (1765–1814), all for whom myth-making belonged to the internal dynamics of a community throughout its historical development.

Berlin's notion of pluralism differs from that of the major Poststructuralist discourses imported into the field of architectural and urban theory, notably those of Deleuze and Guattari. Poststructuralism is an essentially relativist current of philosophy that questions our ability to acquire knowledge. It originated in France after World War II. Poststructuralism seeks to dismantle mythological apparatuses, showing their lack of essential features. This attitude, Berlin would say, assumes that the application of reason on the world of human beliefs will result in its emancipation. But Berlin holds that reason itself, as an attempt to legitimize overarching frameworks of theory about the world of human belief systems, is at fault. Mythologies are inherent and innate. Given two competing belief systems, the most radical deconstruction (or philosophical analysis) will fail to dissolve either one.

What is Berlin's way out? The aim is not to align the differing beliefs, but rather to ease the perpetual negotiation that is necessary to avoid a descent into violence. For Berlin, the only objective, irreducible, and yet incompatible facts were the belief systems and corresponding utopias themselves. The way out of a probable disaster, the prerequisite for a successful ongoing negotiation or armistice, is not reason but the empathetic imagination. Berlin did not deny that identity myths are themselves constructed based on a desire to differentiate from other identity myths; he simply states that this insight simply will do nothing to dissolve these oppositions. Therefore, he proposed the use of imagination to temporarily penetrate into the other's belief system empathetically. Although there is no reconciliation in sight, Berlin hoped to make a truce possible. Although destroying utopia, he proposed to pay tribute to the idea through the technique of empathetic penetration into another's utopia. Berlin's notion of the "uneasy coexistence of incompatible terms," applied to characterize pluralism (a concept critical to the political philosophy of liberalism), was strikingly analogous to the formalist architectural concept of group form.

BERLIN'S ROMANTIC PLURALISM

"What can we be said to owe to Romanticism? A great deal. We owe to Romanticism...the notion that they are many values, and that they are incompatible; the whole notion of plurality, of inexhaustibility, of the imperfection of all human answers and arrangements; the notion that no single answer which claims to be perfect and true, whether in art or in life, can in principle be perfect or true—all this we owe to the Romantics. As a result a rather peculiar situation has arisen. Here are the Romantics, whose chief burden is to destroy ordinary tolerant life...to raise everybody to some passionate level of self-expressive experience, of such a kind as perhaps only divinities, in older works of literature, were supposed to manifest...and yet, as a result of

making clear the existence of a plurality of values,
as a result of driving wedges into the notion of the
classical ideal, of the single answer to all questions,
of the rationalizability of everything, of the whole
jigsaw-puzzle conception of life, they have given promi-
nence to and laid emphasis upon the incompatibility of
human ideals...and so, as a result of this passionate,
fanatical, half-mad doctrine, we arrive at an appreciation of the necessity of tolerating others, of the
impossibility of driving human beings...into the single
solution which possesses us. The result of Romanticism,
then, is liberalism, toleration, decency, and...some
degree of rationalized self-understanding. This was
very far from the intentions of the Romantics...they
were hoist with their own petard. Aiming at one thing,
they produced, fortunately for us all, almost the
exact opposite." [41]

"Pluralism, with the measure of 'negative liberty'
that it entails, seems to me a truer and more humane
ideal than the goals of those who seek in the great
disciplined, authoritarian structures the ideal of
'positive' self-mastery by classes, or peoples, or the
whole of mankind. It is truer because it does, at least,
recognize the fact that human goals are many, not all
of them commensurable, and in perpetual rivalry with
one another. To assume that all values can be graded
on one scale, so that it is a mere matter of inspection
to determine the highest, seems to me to falsify our
knowledge that men are free agents, to represent moral
decision as an operation which a slide-rule could, in
principle, perform. To say that in some ultimate, all-
reconciling, yet realizable synthesis, duty is interest,
individual freedom is pure democracy or an authoritarian
state, is to throw a metaphysical blanket over either
self-deceit or deliberate hypocrisy. It is more humane
because it does not (as the system-builders do) deprive

59

men, in the name of some remote, or incoherent, ideal, of much that they have found to be indispensable to their life as unpredictably self-transforming human beings. In the end, men choose between ultimate values. They choose as they do because their life and thought are determined by fundamental moral categories and concepts that are, at any rate, over large stretches of time and space, a part of their being and thought and sense of their own identity; part of what makes them human. It may be that the ideal of freedom to choose ends without claiming eternal validity for them, and the pluralism of values connected with this, is only the late fruit of our declining capitalist civilization: an ideal which remote ages and primitive societies have not recognized, and one which posterity will regard with curiosity, even sympathy, but little comprehension. This may be so; but no skeptical conclusion seems to me to follow. Principles are not less sacred because their duration cannot be guaranteed. Indeed, the very desire for guarantees that our values are eternal and secure in some objective haven is perhaps only a craving for the certainties of childhood or the absolute values of our primitive past. 'To realize the relative validity of one's convictions,' said an admirable writer of our time, 'and yet to stand for them unflinchingly is what distinguishes a civilized man from a barbarian.'[42] To demand more than this is perhaps a deep and incurable metaphysical need; but to allow it to determine one's practice is a symptom of an equally deep, and more dangerous, moral and political immaturity."[43]

EMPATHY

According to Berlin, people are confined to perspectives that are constrained by myths, and the liberal ideal is the coexistence of such incompatible myths. It follows that empathy is a prerequisite for coexistence. What is empathy, formally speaking, in art and urban design? According to German psychological theorist Robert Vischer (1847–1933), the mind recognizes anthropomorphic features in observed phenomena. In his words, empathy is "the intuited fact that object and self are one."[44] Life properties are perceived to reside in dead objects; fondness for a form is the consequence of a recognition of oneself in it.

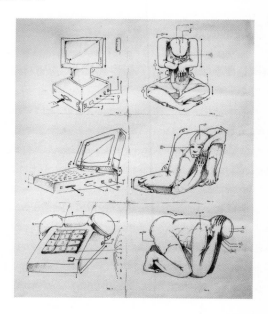

This concept is central in the work of early German art historians. For instance, Heinrich Wölfflin (1864–1945), Giedion's teacher and a Hegelian, saw art progress toward ever higher stages of abstraction in the development of Western art. Nevertheless, he asserted the empathy principle as an a priori of aesthetics. Wilhelm Worringer (1881–1965), a student of Alois Riegl, made a brilliant attempt to relate the two lineages of art history in his

Abstraktion und Einfühlung (1908). In Worringer's view, societies destabilized by change and massive uncertainty produce art that searches for permanence through abstraction. Worringer presented these as two equal poles, but while *einfühlung* (empathy) amounts to the passing of the self into the object, he is in fact saying that *abstraktion* (abstraction) emerges when the self no longer wants to pass into the object.

The slider on a metaphorical bar, hung between the extremes of complete abstraction and total empathy, measures a society's sense of organic identity. The abstract object represents the self as it would like to be rather than as it thinks it is. In effect, Worringer stated that societies in crisis, such as the crisis of modernity, will resort to abstraction as a means to affirm permanence at the very moment when the reality of that society seems to push the stability of its existence completely behind the horizon.

WORRINGER'S "ABSTRACTION" AND "EMPATHY"

"Let us recapitulate: The original artistic impulse has nothing to do with imitation of nature. This impulse is in search of pure abstraction as the sole possibility of finding rest amidst the confusion and obscurity of the image of the world, and it creates a geometric abstraction starting with itself, in a purely instinctive manner. It is the realized expression, and the sole expression conceivable for man, of the emancipation from any arbitrariness and any temporality of the image of the world. But soon this impulse tends to rip out the individual thing from the exterior world, which retains as its main interest its obscure and disconcerting connection with this outside world, and so tries to get closer to it through artistic restitution of its materials individuality, to purify this individual thing of everything that is life and temporality in it, to make it as much as possible independent both from the surrounding world and from the subject of contemplation, which does not want to enjoy in it the vitality that is common to both, but the necessity and the legitimacy where this impulse can find refuge from its connection with ordinary life, in the only abstraction to which it can aspire and which it can attain. Restitution of the finite material individuality is both important and possible underneath the surface boundaries but also in the intermingling of artistic presentation with the rigid world of the crystallo-geometric: namely, the two solutions that we could observe. Anyone who understands his own solutions in the light of all their presuppositions can no longer speak of 'these charming childish mumblings of stylization.' Now, all these momentums that we have just analyzed, and which revealed themselves as so many aspects of the need for abstraction, are what our definition wants to gather and summarize with the help of the notion of 'style,' and what it wants to oppose as such to any Naturalism that results from the need for *Einfühlung* [empathy]. Because the need for *Einfühlung* and the need for abstraction appeared to us as the two poles of man's artistic sensitivity inasmuch as it can be the object of pure aesthetic appreciation. These two needs are antithetical, they exclude each other, and the history of art never ceases to display the continual confrontation between the two tendencies."[45]

ACROPOLIS

The assemblage concept in Surrealist sculpture is a negative aesthetic that uses terms (in this case monuments) out of context, displaced, and in conflict with others, in order to reveal their own limitations and artificiality. By contrast, the liberal idea of assembly is positive, understanding the Group as positive, gathering myths to form an intrinsically pluralistic symbol.

It was during a lecture series at Carnegie Mellon University in the late 1950s that Giedion formulated the concept of "group design."[46] He asserted that all art has an innate drive toward abstraction. He took up the topic of patterns in prehistoric art, first discovered in the caves of Altamira, Spain, in 1879, as a basis and a justification for the abstractions of Modernism. The naturalistic reflex, he argues, was a temporary cultural deviation of the bourgeoisie. The advent of photography, which challenged traditional art's claim to realism, liberated it once more to develop independently. Abstraction speaks to an "eternal present" (a phrase he uses in the title of his lecture series on the cave paintings).[47]

Giedion's analysis of the cave paintings focused on the manner in which the artist(s) juxtaposed and related diverse symbols. Invoking French archaeologist André Leroi-Gourhan (1911–1986), he observed that the position of each ideogram is not random or chaotic; and noting the constant relative position of each ideogram in relation to others in its proximity—notwithstanding the variously oriented drawing surfaces of cave walls, ceilings, and floors—Giedion identified a non-orthogonal compositional order. The ideograms acquire meaning not only because of internal formal structure, such as their realistic content, but also because

This page and next, images reproduced courtesy the Doxiadis Archives and the MIT Press they are part of a syntax based on their relative proximity to other ideograms and their operation as components of a semantic system (the various elements have meaning in relation to each other). For Giedion, the drawings were therefore "intentional groupings, formulas if you will."[48]

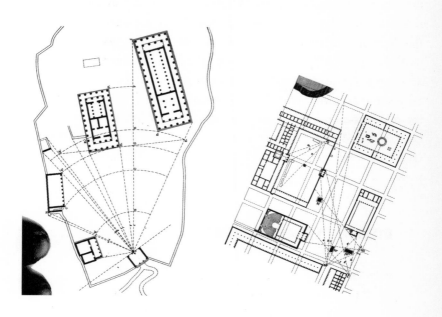

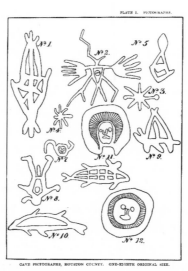

PLATE 1. PICTOGRAPHS.

CAVE PICTOGRAPHS, HOUSTON COUNTY. ONE-EIGHTH ORIGINAL SIZE.

From this starting point, Giedion sought an analogous template in architecture; the Acropolis would emerge, by the end of the decade, as a cornerstone of his group design concept. Berlin's political philosophy of liberalist pluralism corresponds to formal principles of representation in the group form as developed by the protagonists. This is not only a matter of Sert's desire to make forms that are as contrasting as possible, but also of a transposition of the discourse of architectural form from the sphere of technology to that of politics. Although studied by Le Corbusier, the Acropolis as a symbolic form of modern pluralism really gained traction in the postwar years, when the protagonists of the Core, abandoning the machine as metaphor, embraced it as a reference model: Sert often referred to it, Giedion devoted several articles to it, and the Greek architect Konstantinos Doxiadis (1913–1975) wrote his master's thesis about it, which Tyrwhitt would publish in 1972.

GIEDION ON THE ACROPOLIS

"The layout of Greek monumental buildings gives rise
to the freest interplay between their volumes. . . .
The principle of group design is extensively
applied to the planning of the democratic Greek city-
states, where the rights of the individual and the
rights of the community are clearly demarcated.
Group design means that a spatial harmony is set up
between several independent buildings, each of which
has its own formal individuality. . . . The Acropolis
in Athens shows well how group design was used in
the fifth century. Looking inward from the entrance,
the Propylaea, the Parthenon appears as a complete
entity. So does the Erechtheum. From the step of
the Propylaea one sees both standing on the rising
terrain within the same angle of vision."[49]

Group design, as represented in the Greek agora, was
for Giedion a symbolic form of pluralism, and therefore

of the liberal assembly. Norwegian architect Christian Norberg-Schulz (1926–2000) articulated this politico-social model even more artfully:

> "The Greek concept of space, then, is pluralistic... for the Greek space was not one thing, but many, and the Greek language does not have a single word for space. This pluralism was a highly important solution to man's environment, as it liberated man from the fetters of an all-comprehensive system."[50]

AESTHETIC THEORY OF THE MONUMENT

The concept of the symbolic form in Cassirer's writing helps to explain the inspiration behind the Group, for it recurs almost ad nauseam in the protagonists' writings of the 1940s and early 1950s. Cassirer's symbolic form is a mental construct that can be recognized in natural phenomena. Its fundamental content, which he called the "ideational content of the sign," does not depend on its appearance in the world of phenomena, because the content of the symbol is inherently embedded in its ideogrammatic form. It is a diagrammatic form that embeds its own content. The symbolic form is a precast mold that gives a shape to the stream of sensory stimuli. This distinguishes the symbol from the sign, which, for Cassirer, was essentially a Pavlovian reflex mechanism. The sign points directly to a fact of reality, without further mediation; it has no significance within itself. The symbolic form, part of the family of innate forms that are present within us before we experience reality, embodies an abstract kind of understanding.

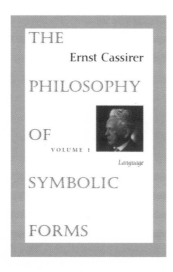

THE
Ernst Cassirer

PHILOSOPHY

OF

VOLUME 1

Language

SYMBOLIC

FORMS

From the moment things enter our consciousness, Cassirer argued, they have left the universe of reality and are formed or molded through the autonomous universe of symbolic forms. Stimuli entering the retina are grafted onto a well-fitting ideogram (or symbolic form) before entering the realm of observations. As molds or as templates, these symbolic forms shape our perception of reality; by extension, they code and structure the totality of expression in human culture.

Evolving from an absolutist viewpoint in Funktionsbegriff und Substanzbegriff (1910) to a much more culture-centered perspective in "Essay on Man" (1944), Cassirer downplayed the absoluteness of symbolic forms and emphasized their ongoing evolution. He saw a sequence of development from myth to science—through religion, art, and language—but these stages coexist as forms of expression, like geological strata. Symbolic forms result from a series of iterations between the templates of the mind, the world of phenomena, and terms of cultural discourse, each influencing and transforming the others with every iteration.

As a result, culture's symbolic forms are caught in a feed-back loop that more or less subjects it to the constraints of its own thinking—to articulate or recognize a symbolic form is to recollect and reorganize the form. Thus history is not merely a record of civilization, it is actively formed, its development etched into its very structure. Cassirer wrote:

> [Symbolic forms in language and myth] are both resolutions of an inner tension, the representation of subjective impulses and excitations in definite objective forms and figures.... [The result being] an abstract-sensuous form.[51]

The symbolic form, understood here as an abstract-sensuous symbol, provides a way out of the dilemma between empathy and abstraction. Empathy lets the self pass into the object, abstraction derives abstract forms from sensory stimuli. Symbolic form is an intersection between these terms. The universe of symbolic forms is an interface between the abstract cognitive work of the mind and the world of phenomena and history. A project for a modern monument, in this sense, is nothing less than these templates of cognition externalized, poured like concrete into pure ideograms of understanding.

CASSIRER'S SYMBOLIC FORMS

"It is characteristic, for example, of the first seemingly naïve and unreflecting manifestations of linguistic thinking and mythical thinking, that they do not clearly distinguish between the content of the 'thing' and the content of the 'sign', but indifferently merge the two. The name of the thing and the thing itself are inseparably fused, the mere word or image contains a magic force through which the essence of the thing gives itself to us. And we need only to transfer this notion from the real to the ideal, from the material to the functional, to find that it contains a kernel of justification. In the immanent development of the mind, the acquisition of the sign really constitutes a first and necessary step toward knowledge of the objective nature of the thing. For consciousness the sign is, as it were, the first stage and the first demonstration of objectivity, because through it the constant flux of the contents of consciousness is for the first time halted, because in it something enduring is determined and emphasized. No mere content of consciousness as such recurs in strictly identical form once it has passed and has been replaced by others. Once it has vanished from consciousness, it is gone forever as that which it was. But to this incessant flux of contents, consciousness now juxtaposes its own unity and the unity of its forms. Its identity is truly demonstrated, not in what it is or has, but in what it does. Through the sign that is associated with the content, the content itself acquires new permanence. For the sign, in contrast to the actual flow of particular contents of consciousness, has a definite ideal meaning, which endures as such. It is not, like the simple given sensation, an isolated particular, occurring but once, but persists as the representative of a totality, as an aggregate of potential contents, beside which it stands as a first 'universal.' In the symbolic function of consciousness—as it operates in language, in art, in myth—certain unchanging fundamental forms, some a conceptual and some of a more sensory nature, disengage themselves from the stream of consciousness; the flux of contents is replaced by a self-contained and enduring unity of form."[52]

SYMBOLIC FORM IN ARCHITECTURE

Our protagonists want Cassirer's template of cognition to be set in concrete. Cassirer was determined to liberate the symbolic form, which originates in mythical thought, from mythical thought itself. That is how we have to understand his intention to treat both mythical thought and the exact sciences with a single theory of form. In order to isolate forms of pure cognition, he needed to strip observations from the flesh of reality and discover the pure ideogram, the template, the element of pure cognition. Cassirer believed that we may be able to recover these templates on their own terms, as autonomous utterances. Architecture conceives of buildings as ideograms of pure cognition, templates of the mind itself.

Cassirer's trilogy lacks a chapter on architecture, but Giedion, Sert, Kahn, and Maki frequently referred to symbolic forms. Their aesthetic project consisted of the externalization of a priori templates of cognition into physical artifacts that will spark a moment of immediate recognition, a flash of empathy with the abstract constructs of the mind itself. As a result, a romanticist-modernist aesthetic is established. In Cassirer's abstract-sensuous schema, cognitive logic and sensuous experience interpenetrate. Art historian Joseph Koerner (b. 1958) dismisses the scientific value of Cassirer's work, describing it instead as an aesthetic project. He describes the Cassirerian aesthetic as sacramental, as it had been for premodern cultures, with their esoteric and undecipherable pictographs, like hieroglyphs.[53] Hence there is a similarity between Romanticism's desire for monuments and symbols, and Modernism's drive for abstraction—first legitimized by functionalist thought, finally defining its own formalist terms as the concrete externalization of pure cognition.

Cassirer, in his efforts to isolate forms of pure cognition, attempted to strip away the images of phenomena that obscure the template itself, those that molded them in the first place. The

72

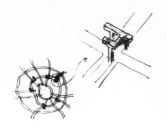

recovery of these templates ought to reveal schemata with an almost timeless depth. Cassirer believed that we may be able to recover these templates on their own terms, as autonomous utterances. The aesthetic experience, then, is triggered through the moment of immediate recognition of the template, observed through the template within the self. Cassirer's project may be described as aimed toward liberating the symbolic form from mythical thought, hence his attempted treatment of both mythical thought and mathematics with a single theory of form. Architecture's project, then, will be the deployment of such forms: buildings as ideograms of pure cognition, templates of the mind itself.

Structuralist linguistics—according to which "the bond between the signifier and signified is arbitrary"—places itself squarely outside of Cassirer's concept of symbolic form.[54] The field of semiotics (the study of signs) had not yet achieved paradigmatic status when Cassirer formulated his theory; but he dismissed it before the fact, asserting that:

73

Measured by the limitless richness and diversity of all intuitive
reality, all [linguistic] symbols would inevitably seem empty;
measured by its individual concretion, they would inevitably
seem abstract and vague…the unity of the sentence…
possesses a definite independent character of "signification."[55]

By the same token, Cassirer's symbolic form has little or
nothing to do with the word "symbolism" as employed in the work
of architects/theorists such as Robert Venturi (b. 1925), Denise
Scott-Brown (b. 1931), or Charles Jencks (b. 1939), these authors
refer to signs or allegories instead of symbols.[56] Nevertheless,
Cassirer's search for a cognitive depth beyond patterns of association produced by culture places him in proximity to Giedion's search
for elements of constancy between prehistory and modernity.

GIEDION'S SYMBOLIC FORMS

As an art historian, Giedion rewrote history as a process of development that would ultimately culminate in a messianic Le Corbusier
as harbinger of architectural liberation through Modernism. In doing
so, he denied other protagonists of expressionist Modernism their
rightful place in the canon of modernist history, such as German
architects Hans Poelzig (1869–1936) and Erich Mendelsohn
(1887–1953).[57] There are family resemblances between the architectural intuitions of later Giedion and Cassirer's symbolic forms.
Introducing his final book, Giedion wrote:

> In the two volumes of The Eternal Present: Beginnings of
> Art and The Eternal Present: Beginnings of Architecture,
> I attempted to get at some fundamental principles. The fore-
> most question was the relation between constancy and change.
> Constancy does not imply mere continuation, but the ability
> of the human mind suddenly to bring life to things that have
> been left slumbering through long ages. [58]

Thus, Giedion's teleology, the goal of his reasoning, begins
to fall into line with Cassirer's, even though they arrived at these
conclusions from greatly distinct traditions. Similarly, there is an
unexpected alignment between the purposes of Wölfflinian formalism (features of style and zeitgeist) and Cassirerian formalism
(features of cognition). Giedion concentrated the bulk of his references under the heading "Annunciation of an Art Historian," which
demonstrated that his sources were the same as Cassirer's.[59]
Giedion also acknowledged Cassirer explicitly in 1962.[60]
 Giedion built a theory of a new monumentality, borne out of his
discovery of an urgent impulse toward abstraction in primitive art.
His purpose was to demonstrate the constancy of the impulse for
abstraction in all forms of human expression, from the very onset
of the history of mankind. This, for him, constituted a fundamental
unity of expression. He organized the history of architecture into

successive space conceptions, which he understood as fundamental
social conceptions of the structure of spatiality itself:

> Man takes cognizance of the emptiness which girds him round
> and gives it a psychic form and expression. The effect of this
> transfiguration, which lifts space into the realm of the emotions,
> is SPACE CONCEPTION [sic]. It is the portrayal of man's inner
> relation to his environment...man thus realizes his urge to
> come to terms with the world.[61]

The space conception is a schema for the fitting of sensory
stimuli into preexisting concepts. In the third-space conception—the
zenith of Giedion's theory of monumentality—Cassirerian symbolic
form as a concept or template is made explicit in the massing of the
building. The inside of the building unites with the outside, establishing a continuous surface that runs through the building. The play
of volumes and spaces, the interweaving of interior and exterior, is
made possible only by high-quality glass and the structural techniques that allow the creation of effective indoor spaces under these
topological conditions. Yet the new monuments derive their authority from the force of primitive forms and symbols—just as artistic
movements like Cubism, Primitivism, and Surrealism had sought to
recall these lingering deep expressions of the precivilized human
mind. The sculptural quality Giedion refers to is identical to that of
an abstract-sensuous symbol.

Untitled, Franz Kline, 1957.

76

In continuous monumentality, architecture finds its vocation: the play of unbroken monumental surfaces, interweaving inside and outside spaces, establishes a three-dimensional gesture. These surfaces wrap around open and closed spaces, public and private. They establish residual volumes, ribbons of form rather than pure objects. These are welded together to become a veritable mute symbol, organizing views and passage, and large open spaces flowing through its own body. In fact, a space that belongs to the public now penetrates all the way into the solid, perforating and shattering its unity. What is left is a monument that frames the public to itself.

GIEDION'S THREE SPACE CONCEPTIONS

The prehistorical conception of space involves an "internal image" in which time is subsumed into space. This intuitive ordering can be found in prehistoric cave paintings, in which a chronological sequence of events and emotions is represented simultaneously, without indication of succession.[62] The first-space conception is expressed in the pyramid, the ziggurat, the totem, and the obelisk, which Giedion calls "space-radiating volumes." They are primary markers, moments of verticality that speak of the power and victory of society over nature, as embodied in the state or ruler. The force of their architecture is directed toward their surroundings.[63] There is no public "inside" to these monuments, because the inside is reserved to central authority: the priests, or the ruler. The territory around the monuments is subjugated to the master volume not only by its sheer height and mass, but also by various landscape and infrastructural devices orienting all toward the single, unifying prism.

The second-space conception corresponds to the possibility of long structural spans, which make monumental interior spaces possible. The great palaces, markets,

and *thermae* of ancient Rome demonstrate an inward-
oriented monumentality. A simple comparison between
the mausoleum for Caesar Augustus and the Pantheon,
both on a circular floor plan, shows what has changed:
the mausoleum is a massive, full cylinder, which
is experienced only from the outside; the Pantheon
is primarily a large indoor space. Giedion associated
this evolution with the rise of a secular mass society which is now allowed into the spaces that were once
reserved for the sacred aristocracy only. This space
conception extends throughout the development of
European civilizations. Gothic, Renaissance, and
Baroque all belong to the second-space conception,
made possible by the twin discoveries of arch and vault.

In the third-space conception, the second is
merged with the first; an architecture of monumental
interiors will merge with the monumental, space-
radiating exterior. A new kind of continuity is
established; the inside of the building is united with
its outside, establishing a continuous surface that
runs through the building and opens the insides of
the monument open to the public. The result is a kind
of simultaneity of previously incongruous elements,
interior and exterior. What Giedion called for
did not yet exist in architecture. He conjured up
an image through writing and assembling disparate
historic images.

SERT'S SYMBOLIC FORMS

Sert's Harvard University Science Center (1968) illustrates his way of deploying sculptural form as a means to organize and clarify the surrounding urban territory. To colonize a part of the town of Cambridge, Massachusetts, for the expanding university, Sert made a gesture to re-define the edge of the campus and assert its identity through form. Built on a T-shaped plan, the building defines an area just beyond the university's historic gated campus. A long wall of offices explicitly outlines the new edge. Its roof is adorned with expressive forms. The figure formed by these elements is complicated by another volume that extends perpendicularly from the middle of the office wall toward the campus yard. It leans, as it were, with its back against the wall, and faces the newly defined public square, between the new building and the old campus. In the Science Center building, Sert transformed and rearranged the formal vocabulary of Modernist architecture into an expressive symbol. A notable change here is in the purpose of such forms. The architecturalization of primitive Surrealist forms results in expressive, vaguely human-like figures, whose position and form simultaneously explain and define the surrounding environment.

Sert's proposal for Welfare (Roosevelt) Island (1970–6) in New York's East River uses anthropomorphic form to humanize the

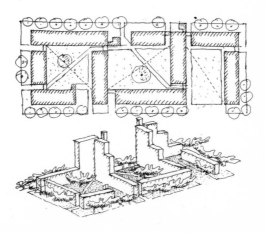

city and make it both legible and accessible to its inhabitants. By fusing aesthetic principles of empathy with the preexisting principle of abstraction, Sert arrived at an architecture of abstract-sensuous forms. It is imperative to distinguish the reading of these projects as symbolic forms from a reading of them as allegorical structures. The symbolic form explains rather than represents. Sert's humanoid gestures explain the city that surrounds it, making it legible, by simultaneously enhancing its structure and crystallizing that structure in a clear symbol.

SERT'S WELFARE ISLAND

Between 1970 and 1976, Sert built about 1,360 apartment units on the island. He designed a series of long, rib-like buildings that cross the island transversely. The linear building plan is complemented by a stepped section, with systematic increases from seven stories at the water's edge to twenty-three stories at the center. The project sets up a schematic topography. Most importantly, with a simple repeated section, this project recapitulates the complex cross-section of neighboring Manhattan, which also builds in height toward the middle of the island. Welfare Island was thus transformed from a residual space, which had hosted, before the housing project, a penitentiary and several other institutional facilities, to a gesture that explains, crystallizes, and enhances the structure of the surrounding city.

Sert's project contrasts starkly with Rem Koolhaas's (b. 1944) New Welfare Island, proposed around the same time and for the same site. Working in a Surrealist manner, Koolhaas proposed a constellation of interventions scattered along the spine of the island. At first glance, the project seems to have potentially accommodated Sert's proposal as one of the diverse objects in the constellation—Koolhaas would propose a similar stepped-up form for the Sphinx Hotel in Times Square—but with a marked difference. Koolhaas's graphic depicts a city made of individual extremes, just barely held together by the grid of Manhattan. When it comes to the island, the individual extremes persist, and minimal cohesion is provided by the concise shape of the island itself. The projects here are "buildings once proposed for New York, but for whatever reason aborted," to be "parked on the blocks to complete the history of Manhattan."[64] The individuality of the interventions dominates.

The architects approached these proposals from two different directions. Koolhaas willed the form to become a diagram of his interpretation of the broader culture of the city in more general terms; Sert willed the form to summarize, crystallize, and explain the geography of the overall city. Koolhaas saw Manhattan as an alignment of insane reactions to the overall order of the grid, which, if they confirm it in the end, form the central concern of his interpretation; Sert saw Manhattan as a global form emerging from the grouping of individual elements. Whereas Koolhaas found the freedom to erect a wild variety of forms, each with its own logic, Sert was convinced of the duty of form to act as a schematic gesture that explains itself and the surrounding territory.

LOUIS KAHN'S SYMBOLIC FORMS

Kahn's paintings of 1948–50 illustrate an architecture of frames and ribbons—not unlike what Giedion called for. Kahn's drawings go farther than his architecture does. Transparency #1 shows a grouping of abstract yet expressive gestures placed in each other's vicinity but unrelated by any apparent geometric order. Like an architectural version of Russian artist El Lissitzky's (1890–1941) Prouns, these are three-dimensional ideograms of architectural elements: a portico, a triangle vaguely resembling a roof, or a corridor; elements of an urban architecture, reduced to their schematic and organizational essence.

What Cassirer tried to do for myth, language, and science, Kahn set out to do for architecture: define a system of essential schemata, form-diagrams that establish the a priori of architectural thinking. To consider the translation of this intention into urban design, we turn to the downtown Philadelphia scheme that Kahn developed between 1951 and 1959. The Philadelphia studies are unique in that they do not answer to a narrowly defined commission. Instead, the architect-planner himself defined the problem—the hollowing-out of central Philadelphia into a formless residue due to the invasion of the automobile—and set out to define the terms of the solution. Kahn's architectural representation of the moment of transition between automobile infrastructure and pedestrian urban space features a series of abstract-sensuous monuments. Placed in each other's vicinity, encircling the downtown pedestrian area, they serve as stations or endpoints of car traffic on the surrounding highways.

"The motor car has completely upset the form of the
city. I feel that the time has come to make the distinction between the Viaduct architecture of the car and
the architecture of man's activities...the Viaduct
architecture enters the city from outlying areas. At
this point, it must become more carefully made and
even at great expense more strategically placed with
respect to the center. The Viaduct architecture includes
the street, which in the center of the city wants to be a
building, a building with rooms below for city piping
services to avoid interruption of traffic when services
need repair. The Viaduct architecture would encompass
an entirely new concept of street movement which distin-
guished between the stop and go staccato of the bus
and from the 'go' movement of the car. They are framing
expressways like rivers. These rivers need harbors.
The interim streets are like canals which need docks.
The harbors are the gigantic gateways expressing the
architecture of stopping. The terminals of the Viaduct
architecture, they are garages in the core, hotels and
department stores around the periphery and shopping
centers on the street floor. This strategic positioning
around the city center would present a logical image
of protection against the destruction of the city
by the motor car. In a sense, the problem of the car and
the city is war, and the planning for the new growth
of cities is not a complacent act, but an act of
emergency....The city [then] would have form."[65]

Kahn's first diagrams contain an analysis of the traffic
flows in place at that time: a series of arrows of varying
thickness, showing a city drowning in a sea of cars.
Following the plan of the American architect Edmund Bacon
(1910-2005), Kahn proposed a more desirable flow

83

of traffic, creating a sizable pedestrian zone in the city. Car traffic flows are concentrated on major arteries adjacent to the city center. In a third step, Kahn defined the moments of the observer's transition from driver to pedestrian along these arteries by drawing a series of solenoid-like spires (rotating arrows going upwards) on the edge between an artery and the pedestrian zone.

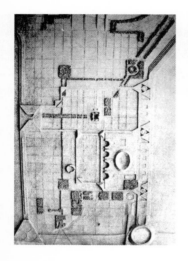

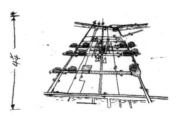

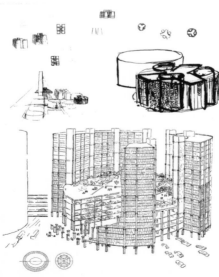

Kahn's proposal celebrates the traffic mode change, clotting it into a series of solemn forms, themselves arranged in a composition that leaves room for each object's individuality. The juxtaposition of forms creates a larger gesture (the encircling/embrace of the city center), thus contributing to the meaning of each constituent form. These are Kahn's symbolic forms for a public architecture for the city. Vaguely resembling an encirclement of monuments, Kahn proposed a different kind of group, where in the middle the fossils of the old city have been saved. Kahn's public architecture emphasizes the very moment of transition between the "Viaduct logic" (of networks and infrastructures) and the place logic (of architecture). He expanded the domain of architecture to include all the clutter and junk that comes with automobile space (exit ramps, garages, gas stations), proceeding to integrate and internalize these within an overall master form. Not merely emblems of a mythical past, his ziggurats and totems effectively transform the perpetual movements of the network society into an eternal arrival. They are symbolic forms of frozen movement, celebrating the moment of stopping rather than the movement itself.

A LIBERAL MONUMENT FOR
A NEW AMERICAN CENTURY?

The contours of a yet unfinished project have by now become visible. Amidst the social changes and Cold War geopolitics of the 1950s, a number of architects and philosophers began to formulate a new political aesthetic. First borne out of a disciplinary reflection about how both architecture and planning could have contributed to warding off the regression of Europe in the 1930s, the project evolved into a celebration of a monument to the values of a liberal political philosophy amidst the sprawling American metropolis. The protagonists understand these values to be in opposition to those of totalitarianism, and in doing so they are bypassing the continental antagonism between fascism and communism.

Beyond the actual political view articulated through form lies a belief that architecture or urban design has the capacity to make a bigger political statement. This disciplinary empowerment stems from the underlying assumption that we understand the world through, at least partially, innate templates of cognition. We can externalize these pure cognitive templates in concrete pieces of architecture. The immediacy of cognition, of identification between one's innate template and the external order observed, yields a moment of aesthetic sublime.

The protagonists' externalized ideogram is a microcosm consisting of a social order based on liberal values. The project foresees a series of dispersed public centers throughout the suburbs, each opposing one another, and each to be formalized differently. The formalism of each rests on the template of the Group: a tight arrangement of a few opposing, non-consensual monuments, denying the city its representation as an organic whole, yet allowing for the disagreement between ideals to be formalized in an almost literal way, crisp, clear and legible.

The alignment of a political ideogram and its celebration into an aesthetic yields the project's fundamental contribution as a political aesthetic. This is what urban design, more than any kind of privately owned and funded architecture has to offer to the world. Nobody may be entitled to make decisions on behalf of the totality, yet every author, architect, and policymaker has the moral duty to declare her intentions on behalf of the whole. The Liberal Monument, as any other urban design template, does just that.

Finally, this projective excavation emphasizes the importance of stating intentions clearly, as they are poured into concrete. This book has not been about post-realization performance, about appropriation by the people, or other measurements of architectural and urban success. History proves that almost any kind of form or building, can, over time, become successful or fail due to actions wholly external to its own constitution. The Liberal Monument is about the empowerment of a discipline using its own means to project and articulate ideals for the whole. Forget the city—the city is now everywhere, everything, and involves almost everyone.

If urban design survives, it will be as a series of non-consensual projects that state their intentions with the greatest formal clarity. One of these is the Liberal Monument. Given that it was never realized, and that the need for a new political aesthetic after the era of unbridled private speculation is clear, this is a call to the new generation to articulate the Liberal Monument for the twenty-first century.

THE CONVERSATION (THAT NEVER TOOK PLACE)

What follows is an imaginary conversation between our protagonists, made conceivable by their implicit agreement. Derived from a rigorous extension of the protagonists' writings, focusing predominantly on unarticulated implications and implicit correspondences, the transcript of such a conversation (which never took place), staged by a time-traveling interviewer, touches on the key concepts of what should be understood as The Liberal Monument.

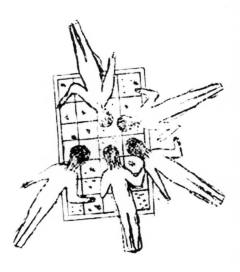

Sert: Progress for architecture will be possible only if we can place it within a larger intellectual project vis-à-vis the current mechanisms of territorial development. "Sprawl," as William Whyte calls this phenomenon in America, is already demonstrating its overwhelming force as a quasi-endless sequence of private developments.[1] I dread the utopianization of this scenario: a "city of tomorrow" formed of endless suburbs, one cottage close to the next, and a helicopter in every backyard.[2] We cannot deny that there is another American culture that is civic and urban. Therefore, I propose the insertion of public devices, devices that civilize the sprawling private territories, in key strategic points within them. I will call these *civic complexes*.[3]

Cassirer: Sert, you sound like a Euro-elitist! Do you want to impose your civilization on others, whom (we have to gather) you consider uncivilized? Stalin's "Palace of the Soviets" was supposed to replicate itself throughout the territories to broadcast the propaganda of a unitary state.[4] Are you proposing the same strategy?

Sert: Not quite. Think about the Acropolis, the Greek concept of democratic space. As Ortega y Gasset said, their revolution has been to define a space amidst the endless fields of nature, defined by its exclusion from the continuum of vegetation.[5] Man erects a space for public discourse. My civic complexes will do the same— they interrupt the continuous stretches of privatized commercial life to introduce a moment of public reflection.

Giedion: I think Sert conceives this separation not literally, as a walled-off space, but figuratively, as a specific recognizable form in the midst of a formless continuum.

Cassirer: But surely you don't believe that the continuum of privatized commercial life is barbarian or vegetative? While the Greeks regarded infinity as negative, formless, and therefore inaccessible to human reason, Giordano Bruno believed the reverse: since Copernicus's heliocentric revolution, infinity has meant the immeasurable and inexhaustible abundance of reality and the unrestricted intellectual power that humans can exercise over it.[6] Sert, you're one revolution behind!

Sert: My claim is just that the Greek spatial revolution was man's setting himself apart from the totality of which he was part. A totality—whether nature for the Greeks, or the state for totalitarian regimes—is a system without a horizon, a continuum from which there is no escape. The endless extension of the posturban sprawling realm suggests a totality. Allow me to draw a parallel between Bruno's view of infinity and Modernist urban planning: Modern planning has declared its purpose to be the efficient organization of territory through functional zoning. In this mode, planning becomes a totalizing endeavor. It takes the entire territory as its scope and applies a single organizing principle all over it. That is the consequence, in our field, of what you call Bruno's positive infinity.

Today the peripheries of cities are expanding so drastically that the cities link up and form a posturban continuum: a system without a horizon, without an escape valve. In this emerging totality, what is lacking is any public moment, defined as a moment in which these dispersed private things become visible simultaneously. Therein lies the purpose of the civic complexes.

Kahn: I agree with Sert. We need a counterproject within the Modern tradition.

Sert: Our purpose is not to plan for a brave new world, but to provide exceptions to it. Havens, if you will.

Giedion: We will need an alliance between architects, artists, planners, and intellectuals!

Cassirer: Sert, many urban intellectuals deplore the civic poverty they perceive in the suburbs. They may support your "havens," but not if they imagine your insertions as monofunctional office districts for public bureaucracies. Would they be wrong?

Sert: Yes. I would like to define "civic space" as an event space in which the unplanned can unfold and where people can freely meet—a space of the unexpected encounter. You know that I have had good conversations with our colleague Le Corbusier on the need for civic centers.[7] But I noticed that he tends to move this complex into a pristine site, as he does with the government complex in his master plan for Chandigarh, where the project then acquires an almost sacral, temple-like quality. This is contrary to civic life as described by Lewis Mumford and William Whyte, and to my own observations of the cities in my native Cataluña, Spain. For the unexpected encounter to occur, different trajectories need to intersect. Different flows of people need to intersect. Therefore, it is absolutely necessary for my civic complex to be embedded in its surroundings. Surrounding streets, flows of people, and roads ought to be addressed in and through the project.

Kahn: Perhaps we can push this even further. Studying Philadelphia, I have been shocked by the extent to which the assault of automobile networks and infrastructures is destroying everything that we value about civic space. Highways and parking lots are being designed from the narrow standpoint of engineering efficiency only. The great promise for a new modernity that they contain remains untapped. The great train stations of the nineteenth century were conceived as monuments to the modernity of this era. Can the parking garages, exit ramps, and traffic junctions become the monuments for our time? The crucial task is to organize the moment of transition from car or train to pedestrian into a grand civic moment. Sert's civic complexes should be such gateways. These *transfer stations* will become actual nodes where flows are transubstantiated, where they mutate. At the point of this metamorphosis from automobile to pedestrian, we as architects will be able to define a civic moment.

Sert: I want to add some contextual intelligence to the civic complex. It should bolt together disparate developments in its vicinity. We all know how suburban development takes place: five hundred homes here, a commercial zone there, and a shopping center across from the motorway. This is the debris of the city, thrown out over the countryside. But through a strategic choice of location, we may transform some of the leftover terrain between these private developments into a developmental interface.

Giedion: Your statements prove that the civic complex is not some nostalgic surrogate or copy of the historic city center.

Cassirer: Interesting, but my concerns are not assuaged yet. What are the functions of the civic complex?

Sert: We want to appropriate the shopping paradigm. With the ascent of the middle classes, a consumption-driven economy is emerging as our predominant one. We should use this force of development to propel the project of the civic complex forward with updated definitions of public space. Take, for instance, a combination of shopping with a movie theater, a hotel, offices, apartments, a post office, and a conference facility. We want the private sector to build this, but in a manner that maximizes its public character and accessibility. The orchestration of these programs is the task of the public sector. It can be achieved through infrastructure design, a formal master plan, or a regulatory framework. This new toolbox will be studied in the Urban Design program I have started at Harvard.

Cassirer: This sounds like something I would agree with. For liberal philosophers, true democracy is a perpetual negotiation of ongoing conflicts of interest. There is no separate, legitimate public except for the ad hoc organizations in which the citizens and interest groups arrange themselves. The public emerges where private interests collide or align; accordingly, the only task of public administration is to guarantee a neutral staging area for negotiation. Isaiah Berlin and I agree that this is the only foundation of the state that can resist regression into fascism. Is this your view, too?

Sert: Yes, it is, and that is why I quoted Ortega y Gasset earlier. I believe he belongs in your line-up. And this political theory of the state (or public government) implies a concept of space that would be closely aligned with Whyte's concept of the urban: the exposure of oneself to difference, to others, *a density of different desires*.

Sert: What's the bottom line here? What is the form of an architecture defined by this public function?

Giedion: The available typologies for a public architecture, delivered to us through European history, has been inextricably tied to the ideology of the church or the state. It is our task now to translate the people's eternal need for symbols into a new monumentality that will respond to the utopias of the citizens and interest groups, rather than the state. The demand for monumentality cannot be suppressed. It tries to find an outlet at all costs. If liberalism ignores this, it will fail to channel a very potent and dangerous desire for identity. So we faced the popular support for false monumentality, figuration, and Neoclassicism in totalitarian regimes, whilst we ourselves engaged in the suppression of figurative representations in the West.

Cassirer: I'm convinced that the basic function of human culture is to symbolize: to make sensory reality understandable by transforming its appearances into cognizable forms of the mind. I have called them *symbolic forms*. They are a series of protolinguistic diagrams, templates that embed their content in their form. They explain rather than represent (the function of an image) or point to something else (the function of a sign). These forms are at once abstract and sensuous. You are proposing to transport these schemata of the mind directly into concrete matter, with the least amount of mediation.

Kahn: I believe we read these forms in even the most banal routines and man-made things. Everything shimmers with an implicitly stated, underlying ideal diagram. It is the architect's task to excavate this ideal (if latent) form. Thus, we are part of the same project—your

94

approach from the philosophy of knowledge, mine from art and architecture!

Maki: These forms are discovered rather than invented; in a sense, they belong to society even before the designer discovers them. What I like about the idea of symbolic forms is that it lifts the making of forms for the city out of the realm of subjectivity. For if I understand Cassirer well, his symbolic forms are collectively understood within a culture, and therefore objective to it. That is why I call them *collective forms*.

Giedion: For me, an architecture of symbolic forms corresponds to a new kind of monumentality, one that belongs to humanism instead of to an ideology of the state. This new monumentality will be mythologizing man's will for emancipation. The first modernists surrendered the mythologizing force of the architectural monument by attempting to achieve absolute abstraction. As a result, we have created architecture and urbanism that are silent, allowing the ruling elite to abuse their capacity to speak. Let us take back architectural speech and use it to address popular culture directly.

Cassirer: The French anthropologist Edmund Doutté once called myth "le désir collectif personnifié," which we could translate as "the collective desire condensed in a human figure"—that, for me, says it all. Man's first emotional utterances (cries, screams, etc.) are transformed into bodily gestures and facial expressions, which become symbols explaining a state of mind. These are then projected onto the surrounding world. The world is thus transformed into a series of physiognomic forms, performing a pantomime. In this world we cannot speak of things in terms of dead or alive. All objects are benign or malignant, friendly or inimical, familiar or uncanny, alluring and fascinating or repellent and threatening. Primitive man is radically united with his world, dissolving in it. This primal layer of understanding is still with us today and resurfaces when distanced logical thought is switched off. In other words, with a disinterested gaze, we are already on the verge of entering the world as a mythical universe of gestures. Architecture as a myth-project is the materialization of these gestures as three-dimensional forms. It follows that the elevations and sections of the project become of utmost importance.

Sert: An architecture of gestural forms means a series of abstract/ empathetic forms that explain the surrounding city!

Giedion: I agree. In my studies on monumentality throughout the development of Western architecture, one element always stands out, namely verticality, confirming Cassirer's suggestion that a public architecture involves the problem of the elevation. You know my obsession with the definition of a new monumentality in architecture—I also call it the *third-space conception*. I conceive of the third-space conception as a synthesis between the first- and second-space conception. The first-space conception is an architecture of pyramids, ziggurats, obelisks, etc.: massive forms whose force is predominantly geared toward the organization and definition of the spaces that are surrounding it. In the second- space conception, architecture's vertical force is geared inwards, toward the monumentalization of its interiors. Now, the third-space conception, the new monumentality, is a synthesis. Here, the vertical force continues from the inside to the outside. We are arriving at a new generation of architectural forms where the space is flowing through the building, from its exteriors and surroundings, through its inner core, to the other sides. The elevations are opened up, a new level of transparency is achieved, there are continuous surfaces uniting the inside to the outside.

Sert: Your prophecy implies that on the horizontal surface, a series of continuously flowing spaces are defined, that pass by, through,

96

and under the form. As a result, a new aesthetic of public space is established that gives very precise definitions of this space.

Kahn: Another breakthrough is that we are now finally abandoning the structure-ornament distinction, which has impeded our discussions on Modern architecture. Instead, the newly found public purpose of architecture leads to a different dichotomy: between gestural force and internal organization; between the demands for a monumental, articulated public presence of architecture, and the resulting pressures on the internal programs and efficiency that justify the building in the first place.

Giedion: This new monumental symbol will be our answer to the Soviet palace.

Maki: Hold on there, Giedion! If we conceive the civic complex as a giant powerful symbol, we are forcing a diverse people into a unified whole—just like the totalitarian regimes of the 1930s—and we won't do justice to our own principles.

Cassirer: But what constitutes the people? We agreed that the public is constituted by an extremely diverse set of groups and individuals who adhere to different worldviews, have different aspirations and utopias, and defend different interests. If this is the public, how can we conceive of its symbolic form?

Giedion: To answer this I'll just point to the concept of the Group. It can be seen in the juxtaposition and superimposition of entirely different and unrelated items in Surrealist art. Take the artist Alberto Giacometti's <u>Projet Pour Une Place</u> (Project for a Plaza), for instance: a series of freestanding symbolic forms placed on a platform, without any clear geometrical relation. The Group approach, which was meant to assert a critique of the objects of capitalism, holds promise as a symbolic form for liberal democracy.

That can be seen if we compare the Surrealist grouping to the Greek Acropolis, one of the first examples of group design. Instead of a single unifying vision, there are different viewpoints, and from each viewpoint one sees at least two or three different monuments, against a background of nature. In it, a plurality of interests together constitutes the collective. The Surrealist assemblage resembles the liberal democratic assembly—its (negative) representation of a perpetual conflict of interest can be the basis for (positive) liberal formal aesthetics.

  Briefly compare architect Boris Iofan's drawings of the Soviet Palace to Giacometti's sculpture Palace at 4 A.M. What kind of palace do you think he is referring to? At night, Stalin is haunted by the fact that there is no singly unifying synthesis, as promised by the template of Iofan's palace. Quite to the contrary, in Giacometti's artwork the different interests and contradictions come to the surface again.

Cassirer: So the form of the civic complex is made up of a juxtaposition and superimposition of different monumental symbols. Each has its own aspirations and purpose, each points to a certain kind of utopia, which is nevertheless made impossible by the presence of other ones nearby?

Giedion: Exactly.

Maki: That makes sense to me. The collective cannot be expressed in a single architectural form, for architecture is a language that has already exhausted itself by doing too much speaking. Instead, the contours of a collective form will be found exactly in this grouping of different symbols. Through the juxtaposition and super-imposition of two forms, a third form will implicitly emerge. Only urban design is sensitive to this aesthetic, because it emerges between buildings.

Sert: Let us be clear: this grouping will consist of architecture, but also of landscape forms and even infrastructure forms.
Let us restate our purpose here: to build a definition of architecture by placing it in the service of a larger project vis-à-vis the current mechanisms of urban development. This project, called the Liberal Monument, defines architecture purely from the point of view of its public function. Its template is that of a grouping of monumental symbols, and together they establish the civic complex, a symbolic form of liberal democracy. If we are in agreement, I suggest we write this out in a manifesto and propose it as a new project within the modern movement. Are you with me?

Kahn, Cassirer, Maki, Giedion: Yes.

POSTSCRIPT: RECENT EXERCISES

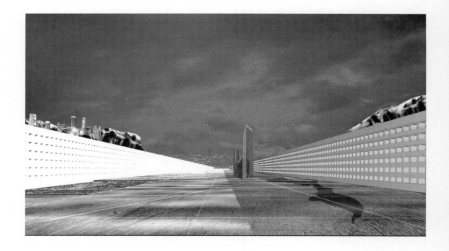

A hypothetical B-movie scenario for Los Angeles after suffering a devastating earthquake. The city's rebirth as three islands with golden beaches, west of a reconfigured American West Coast, features an ever-changing collection of monuments drawn in the sand. Academic speculation, Cambridge, MA, 2000.

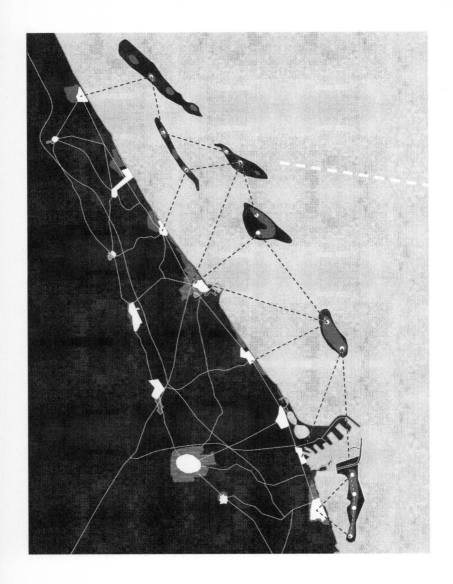

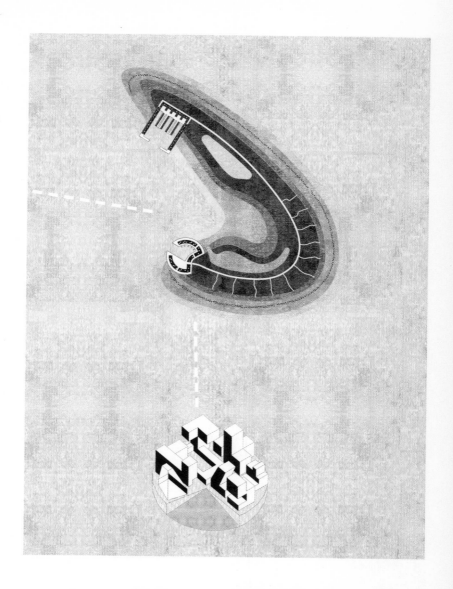

opposite and above: A 100-year plan for a series of islands of the Flemish coast. The islands are shifting sandbanks in a dynamic, maritime environment. However, a constellation of concrete drums will stay in place and anchor a coastal defense system while allowing civilization to leave its footprint. Designed by ORG Office for Permanent Modernity, with IMDC, ATM, Arcadis, Deme, and Denul, 2008–2010.

opposite and above: Project for the conversion of Reykjavik's national airport. One landing strip is the length of the city's main shopping street. Doubling the downtown area by inserting an additional, equally sized civic core atop the tarmac results in a large, territorial figure; a chain of civic cores and monumental buildings. Design study by ORG Office for Permanent Modernity.

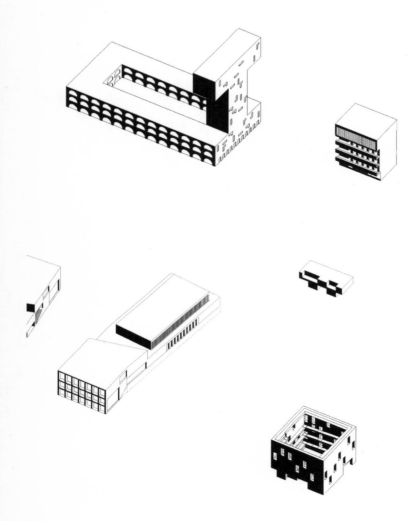

above and opposite: Exercises in Empathy: Building designs for a series of projects in Belgium, drawn as single-cell organisms stuck mid-motion. The projects include a library, a hotel, residences, a town square, and an apartment complex, some have been realized. Projects by ORG Office for Permanent Modernity.

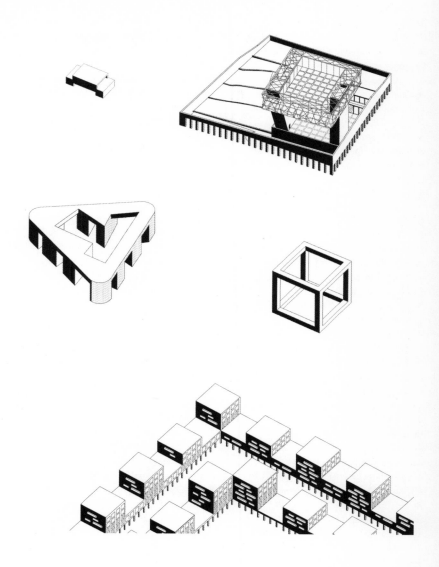

Postscript credits: ORG Office staff/partners i.r.t projects: Luk Peeters, Natalie Seys, Alexander D'Hooghe, Oliver Wuttig, James D. Graham, Wim Francois, Tien-Yun Lee, James Shen, Andrew Corrigan, Shirley Shen, and Lizzie Krasner.

NOTES

1 William Whyte, "Are Cities Un-American?" The Exploding Metropolis (1957).

2 As portrayed in Frank Lloyd Wright's Broadacres project drawings.

3 As described in Josep Lluís Sert, "Urban Design" (lecture, AIA Regional Conference of the Middle Atlantic District, October 23, 1953), 4–5.

4 Designed by Boris Iofan as the winning entry for the international competition for the Palace of the Soviets (1931–34).

5 José Ortega y Gasset, The Revolt of the Masses (New York: W. W. Norton & Company, 1932), 153–4.

6 Ernst Cassirer, An Essay on Man (New Haven, CT: Yale University Press, 1944), 14–15. Cassirer explores this shift in the appreciation of the infinite (from negative to positive) through some readings from the fifteenth to the eighteenth century.

7 These discussions are apparent in their collaboration for the master plan for Bogota (1951–1952), where they both drew conflicting versions of a civic center or complex, but both Sert and Le Corbusier include it centrally in the plan.

8 Sigfried Giedion, "The Need for a New Monumentality." Harvard Architecture Review (1984): 53–61. See also Joan Ockman and Edward Eigen, eds., Architecture Culture 1943–1968: A Documentary Anthology (New York: Rizzoli, 1993), 29–30.

9 John Stuart Mill, "Bentham" London and Westminster Review (April 1836): .

10 Jürgen Habermas, The Structural Transformation of the Public Sphere, trans. Thomas Burger and Frederick Lawrence (Cambridge, MA: MIT Press, 1989).

11 Ibid., 137.

12 Manfredo Tafuri, Architecture and Utopia: Design and Capitalist Development, trans. Barbara Luiga La Penta (Cambridge, MA: MIT Press, 1976), 36–7.

13 Trevor Pateman, "Majoritarianism: An Argument from Rousseau and Condorcet,"Cogito 2, no.3 (1988): 29–31. A term developed by Trevor Pateman.

14 Karl Marx, "Critique of the Gotha Programme," in Selected Works (Moscow: Progress Publishers, 1970), 3, 13–30; Alexis de Tocqueville, "Unlimited Power of the Majority in the United States, and its Consequences," in Democracy in America, trans. A. Goldhammer (New York: Library of America, 2004).

15 Bernard Rudofsky, Architecture without Architects: An Introduction to Non-Pedigreed Architecture (New York: Museum of Modern Art, 1964). This book is the catalog to an exhibition Rudofsky curated at MOMA with the same title.

16 In Russia this included Viktor Shklovsky (1893–1984) and Boris Eichenbaum (1886–1959), and in the United States, among others, Clement Greenberg (1909–1994) and the postwar generation of abstract expressionists and minimalist artists.

17 OMA was the practice and vehicle for the ideas of the celebrated, maverick Dutch architect Rem Koolhaas (b. 1944). For an example of OMA's work, see the massive China Central Television (CCTV) headquarters in Beijing.

18 Louis Kahn, "Talk at the Conclusion of the Otterlo Congress," in CIAM 59 in Otterlo, ed. Oscar Newman (Stuttgart: Karl Kramer, 1961), 207.

19 Josep Lluís Sert, "Urban Design" at the 1953 AIA Regional Conference.

20 Ibid.

21 Ortega y Gasset, The Revolt of the Masses, 153–154.

22 Jacqueline Tyrwhitt, "Cores within the Urban Constellation," in CIAM 8—The Heart of the City: Towards the Humanisation of Urban Life, ed. Josep

Lluís Sert and Ernesto Nathan Rogers (London: Lund Humphries, 1952), 104.

23 Hans Blumenfeld, "Continuity and Change in Urban Form," Journal of Urban History 1, no.2 (February 1975): .

24 Patrick Geddes, City Development: A Report to the Carnegie Dunfermline Trust (New Jersey: Rutgers University Press, 1904). Also see the Strathclyde University Archives, where all Tyrwhitt's papers are held. This collection contains all correspondence with her mentor Patrick Geddes. Geddes's work on the polynuclear territory was published first as City Development. Lewis Mumford amplified and popularized Geddes's work in the United States.

25 Walter Christaller, The Central Places of Southern Germany (Englewood Cliffs, NJ: Prentice-Hall, 1966).

26 August Lösch, The Economics of Location (New Haven, CT: Yale University Press, 1954).

27 Jean Gottmann, Megalopolis: The Urbanized Northeastern Seaboard of the United States (Cambridge, MA: MIT Press, 1961). Gottman's Megalopolis united Christaller's interurban and Lösch's intraurban logics, and was roughly contemporary to Tyrwhitt's work. The concept of megalopolis corresponds to Gottmann's assertion that several adjacent and increasingly overlapping metropolitan regions should be read as a single system, erasing the historical distinction between city and countryside.

28 Manuel de Sola-Morales, ed., "The Periphery," Urbanismo Revista 9–10 (1992): 4–5.

29 Ibid.

30 Manuel de Sola-Morales, "Designing Cities," Lotus Quaderni Documents 23 (1999): 72.

31 André Breton, "Secrets of the Magical Surrealist Art," in Manifestoes of Surrealism (Ann Arbor: University of Michigan Press, 1969), 35. Describing Surrealist dialogue, the French writer and poet André Breton (1896–1966) said, "The remarks exchanged are not, as is generally the case, meant to develop some thesis, however unimportant it may be... the words, the images are only so many springboards for the listener."

32 Theodor Adorno, "Looking Back on Surrealism," in Notes to Literature (New York: Columbia University Press, 1991), 87. According to Adorno (1903–1969), "There is a shattering and regrouping, but no dissolution....The subject is at work much more openly...in Surrealism than in the dream."

33 Rosalind Krauss, "Photographic Conditions of Surrealism," in The Originality of the Avant-Garde and Other Modernist Myths (Cambridge, MA: MIT Press, 1985), 107.

34 Fumihiko Maki and Masato Ohtaka, "Collective Form: Three Paradigms," in Investigations in Collective Form (St. Louis, MO: School of Architecture, Washington University, 1964), 20.

35 Umberto Eco, The Open Work, trans. Anna Cancogni (Cambridge, MA: Harvard University Press, 1989).

36 Kenneth Frampton, "Thoughts on Fumihiko Maki," The Pritzker Architecture Prize, http://www.pritzkerprize.com/laureates/1993/essay.html. The connection made by Kenneth Frampton is being evoked here: "[Rather than indulging in iconographic excesses] his work is informed by a disconcerting and contradictory combination of anxiety and optimism. On the one hand he remains extremely skeptical, while, on the other, he projects the Blochian idea of hope; the famous 'not yet' of the Weimar Republic."

37 Isaiah Berlin, "The Apotheosis of Romantic Will: The Revolt Against the Myth of an Ideal World," in The Crooked

Timber of Humanity, ed. Henry Hardy (New York: Knopf, 1991), 236–7.

38   Ernst Cassirer, The Myth of the State (New Haven, CT: Yale University Press, 1946).

39   Ibid., 280. Cassirer builds this definition based on ideas of the French anthropologist Edmond Doutté; Edmond Doutté, Magie et Réligion dans L'Afrique du Nord (Paris: Maisonneuve/Geuthner, 1984).

40   Isaiah Berlin, "Philosophy and Government Repression," in The Sense of Reality: Studies in Ideas and Their History (New York: Farrar, Straus, and Giroux, 1998), 54–76; José Ortega y Gasset, "The Greatest Danger: The State," in The Revolt of the Masses, 115–24.

41   Isaiah Berlin, "The Lasting Effects," in The Roots of Romanticism, ed. Henry Hardy (Princeton, NJ: Princeton University Press, 1999), 146–47.

42   Joseph Schumpeter, Capitalism, Socialism and Democracy (London: Allen & Unwin, 1943), 243.

43   Isaiah Berlin, "Two Concepts of Liberty," in The Proper Study of Mankind: An Anthology of Essays, ed. Henry Hardy (New York: Farrar, Straus, and Giroux, 1998), 242.

44   From a summary of Vischer's writing (in German), in Charles Edward Gauss, "Empathy," in The Dictionary of the History of Ideas, vol. 2, Studies of Selected Pivotal Ideas, ed. Philip P. Wiener (New York: Charles Scribner's Sons, 1973–4), 86–9.

45   Excerpt from a translation of Wilhelm Worringer's text, in Jean-Louis Ferrier, Yann le Pichon, and Walter D. Glanze, Art of Our Century: The Chronicle of Western Art, 1900 to the Present (New York: Prentice-Hall, 1988), 94.

46   Sigfried Giedion, Architecture and the Phenomena of Transition: The Three Space Conceptions in Architecture, ed.

Jacqueline Tyrwhitt (Cambridge, MA: Harvard University Press, 1971), 270–4.

47   Sigfried Giedion, The Eternal Present in Art: A Contribution on Constancy and Change (New York: Bollingen Foundation, 1962), 245.

48   Ibid.

49   Sigfried Giedion, The Beginnings of Architecture (New York: Bollingen Foundation, 1964).

50   Christian Norberg-Schulz, Meaning in Western Architecture (New York: Rizzoli, 1974), 39.

51   Ernst Cassirer, Language and Myth, trans. Susanne Langer (New York: Dover, 1946), 88.

52   Ernst Cassirer, The Philosophy of Symbolic Form, part 1: Language, ed. Charles Wendel (New Haven, CT: Yale University Press, 1955).

53   Joseph Leo Koerner, review of Perspective as Symbolic Form, by Erwin Panovsky, The New Republic (April 26, 1993).

54   Lois Tyson, Critical Theory Today: A User-Friendly Guide (New York: Garland, 1999), 197–200.

55   Cassirer, Philosophy of Symbolic Forms, 108.

56   Robert Venturi, Denise Scott-Brown, and Steven Izenour, eds., Learning From Las Vegas (Cambridge, MA: MIT Press, 1976); Robert Venturi and Denise Scott-Brown, Architecture as Signs and Systems for a Mannerist Time (Cambridge, MA: Belknap Press, 2004); and Charles Jencks, The Language of Post-Modern Architecture (New York: Rizzoli, 1977). Venturi, Scott-Brown, and Jencks shaped American architectural culture in its turn away from abstraction, towards explicit, literal, and figurative signs. They did so with the argument that pop art and popular culture needed to be brought into high architectural discourse.

57   There is little left as built legacy of the amazing œuvre of these architects in their expressionistic phase. Poelzig's most well-known contribution is his design for the Grosses Schauspielhaus in Berlin from 1919. Mendelsohn's most iconic expressionistic building is the Eisensteinturm, but projects like the 'German Workers Union' and the 'Columbus Haus' translate an expressionistic sensitivity into a clear, radical and precise urban plan that contextualizes expression in order to clarify the surrounding city and make it legible.

58   Sigfried Giedion, Architecture and the Phenomena of Transition: The Three Space Conceptions in Architecture (Cambridge, MA: Harvard University Press, 1971)

59   Giedion, The Eternal Present: The Beginnings of Art, 40.

60   Ibid., 82–5.

61   Giedion, Architecture and the Phenomena of Transition.

62   Ibid., 520.

63   Giedion, The Beginnings of Architecture, 2.

64   Ibid., 301.

65   Louis Kahn, "Form and Design," in Essential Texts, ed. Robert Twombly, (New York: W. W. Norton & Company, 2003), 73–4.

ACKNOWLEDGMENTS

This book was originally a 450-page doctoral manuscript, prepared at Berlage Institute and the Delft University of Technology. I am extremely grateful to Shantel Blakely, who did invaluable and fundamental editorial work in helping reduce this manuscript to its manifesto size. However, I wish to especially thank my promoters Wiel Arets and Jurgen Rosemann, as well as committee members Marcel Smets, Rem Koolhaas, and Alex Krieger, for their invaluable criticism of the project. I am also grateful to Roemer van Toorn and Piero Vittorio Aureli for our productive exchanges; and to Rob Docter for his unfailing support of the project and committment to see it completed. Finally, I am grateful to a broader community of peers who have been willing to comment and critique the work as it developed in its various stages, without a formalized institutional role: Steve Swiggers, Jan Mannaerts, Geert Antonissen, Talia Dorsey, Kersten Geers, Hashim Sarkis, Richard Sommer, Veronique Patteeuw, Vincent Brunetta, Silvia Benedito, Ana Miljacki, Natalie Seys, Arjen Oosterman and Ole Bouman. The support of Henry Ng, Nancy Eklund Later, Lauren Nelson-Packard, and Salomon Frausto in the editorial stage has been substantive. Work and the drawings in this project began in 2000 at the GSD, they were formalized as a PhD dissertation in November 2002. By February 2005, the project was formally completed, although editing continued until February 2008. The dissertation itself was defended in November 2007.